The Evil *and the* Guilty

The Evil and the Guilty

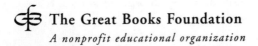 The Great Books Foundation
A nonprofit educational organization

Published and distributed by

⊖ **The Great Books Foundation**
A nonprofit educational organization

35 East Wacker Drive, Suite 2300
Chicago, IL 60601-2298

First Printing
9 8 7 6 5 4 3 2 1 0

Library of Congress Cataloging-in-Publication Data
The Evil and the guilty
    p.   cm. — (50th anniversary series)
    Contents: After the ball / Leo Tolstoy — On evil, guilt, and power / Friedrich
Nietzsche — Moosbrugger / Robert Musil — The sorcerer's apprentice / Charles
Johnson — Stavrogin's confession / Fyodor Dostoevsky — Poetry / Samuel Taylor
Coleridge — Questions for Coup de grâce (Marguerite Yourcenar) — Questions
for Philadelphia fire (John Edgar Wideman)
    ISBN 1-880323-80-X
    1. Literature — Collections. 2. Group reading. 3. Reader-response criticism.
I. Great Books Foundation (U.S.)   II. Series: Great Books Foundation 50th
anniversary series.
PN6014.E85   1997
808.8—DC21   97-42333

CONTENTS

"So that's what Nietzsche means when he says that higher culture is based on the spiritualization of cruelty!" "Why does Moosbrugger feel an overwhelming temptation to go for his knife when he is unable to hold the world together?" "Does good become evil if one is too faithful or too eager?"

Anyone who has been in a book discussion group has experienced the joy of new insight. Sometimes an idea or question occurs to us during the group meeting. Often, it is afterward—sometimes much later—that an idea we had overlooked unexpectedly strikes us with new force. A good group becomes a community of minds. We share perspectives, questions, insights, and surprises. Our fellow readers challenge and broaden our thinking as we probe deeply into characters and ideas. They help us resolve questions, and raise new ones, in a creative process that connects literature with life.

It is this kind of experience that makes book discussion groups worthwhile, and that the Great Books Foundation fosters for thousands of readers around the world.

The Great Books Foundation is a pioneer of book discussion groups that bring together dedicated readers who wish to continue to learn throughout their lives. The literature anthologies published by the Foundation have been the focus of many enlightening discussions among people of all educational backgrounds and walks of life. And the *shared inquiry* method practiced by Great Books groups has proven to be a powerful approach to literature that solves many practical concerns of new discussion groups: How can we maintain a flow of ideas? What kinds of questions should we discuss? How can we keep the discussion focused on the reading so that we use our time together to really get at the heart of a work—to learn from it and each other?

With the publication of its 50th Anniversary Series, the Great Books Foundation continues and expands upon its tradition of helping all readers engage in a meaningful exchange of ideas about outstanding works of literature.

ABOUT *THE EVIL AND THE GUILTY*

The reading selections in *The Evil and the Guilty* have been chosen to stimulate lively shared inquiry discussions. This collection brings together works from around the world that speak to each other on a theme of universal human significance. In this volume you will find classic works by Friedrich Nietzsche, Leo Tolstoy, and Fyodor Dostoevsky; a selection from the monumental novel *The Man Without Qualities* by Robert Musil; contemporary fiction by African American author Charles Johnson; and poetry by Samuel Taylor Coleridge.

These are carefully crafted works that readers will interpret in different ways. They portray characters whose lives and motivations are complex, embody concepts that go beyond simple analysis, and raise many questions to inspire extended reflection.

As an aid to reading and discussion, open-ended *interpretive questions* are included with each selection in the volume, and also for the recommended novels *Coup de Grâce* by Marguerite Yourcenar and *Philadelphia Fire* by John Edgar Wideman. A fundamental or *basic* interpretive question about the meaning of the selection is printed in boldface, followed by a list of related questions that will help you fully discuss the issue raised by the basic question. Passages for *textual analysis* that you may want to look at closely during discussion are suggested for each set of questions. Questions under the heading "For Further Reflection" can be used at the end of discussion to help your group consider the reading selection in a broader context.

ABOUT SHARED INQUIRY

The success of Great Books discussions depends not only on thought-provoking literature, but also on the shared inquiry method of discussion. A shared inquiry discussion begins with a basic interpretive question—a genuine question about the meaning of the selection that continues to be puzzling even after careful reading. As participants offer different possible answers to this question, the discussion leader or members of the group follow up on the ideas that are voiced, asking questions about how responses relate to the original question or to new ideas, and probing what specifically in the text prompted the response.

In shared inquiry discussion, readers think for themselves about the selection, and do not rely on critical or biographical sources outside the text for ideas about its meaning. Discussion remains focused on the text. Evidence for opinions is found in the selection. Because interpretive questions have no single "correct answer," participants are encouraged to entertain a range of ideas. The exchange of ideas is open and spontaneous, a common search for understanding that leads to closer, more illuminating reading.

Shared inquiry fosters a habit of critical questioning and thinking. It encourages patience in the face of complexity, and a respect for the opinions of others. As participants explore the work in depth, they try out ideas, reconsider simple answers, and synthesize interpretations. Over time, shared inquiry engenders a profound experience of intellectual intimacy as your group searches together for meaning in literature.

IMPROVING YOUR DISCUSSIONS

The selections in *The Evil and the Guilty* will support six meetings of your discussion group, with each selection being the focus of a single meeting. Discussions usually last about two hours, and are guided by a member of the group who acts as leader. Since the leader has no special knowledge or qualification beyond a genuine curiosity about the text, any member of the group may lead discussion. The leader carefully prepares the interpretive questions that he or she wants to explore with the group, and is primarily responsible for continuing the process of questioning that maintains the flow of ideas.

To ensure a successful discussion, we encourage you to make it a policy to read the selection twice. A first reading will familiarize you with the plot and ideas of a selection; on a second reading you will read more reflectively and discover many aspects of the work that deepen your thinking about it. Allowing a few days to pass between your readings will also help you approach a second reading with greater insight.

Read the selection actively. Make marginal comments that you might want to refer to in discussion. While our interpretive questions can help you think about different aspects of the work, jotting down your own questions as you read is the best way to engage with the selection and bring a wealth of ideas and meaningful questions to discussion.

During discussion, expect a variety of answers to the basic question. Follow up carefully on these different ideas. Refer to and read from the text often—by way of explaining your answer, and to see if the rest of the group understands the author's words the same way you do. (You will often be surprised!) As your group looks closely at the text, many new ideas will arise.

While leaders in shared inquiry discussion strive to keep comments focused on the text and on the basic interpretive question the group is discussing, the entire group can share responsibility for politely refocusing comments that wander from the text into personal anecdotes or issues that begin to sidetrack discussion.

Remember that during shared inquiry discussion you are investigating differing perspectives on the reading, not on social issues. Talk should be about characters in the story, not about participants' own lives. By maintaining this focus, each discussion will be new and interesting, with each participant bringing a different perspective to bear on the text. After the work has been explored thoroughly on its own terms, your thinking about important issues of the day or in your own life will be enhanced. We have found that it is best to formally set aside a time—perhaps the last half-hour of discussion or over coffee afterward—for members of the group to share personal experiences and opinions that go beyond a discussion of the selection.

DISCUSSING THE POETRY SELECTION

Many book groups shy away from the challenge of discussing poetry, but the shared inquiry method will enable you to make poetry a very satisfying part of your discussion group. Poetry, by its very nature, communicates ideas through suggestion, allusion, and resonance. Because meaning in poetry resides in the interaction between author and reader, and is brought to light through the pooling of different perspectives and readers' responses, poems are ideal for shared inquiry discussion.

It is helpful to read the poem, or parts of it, aloud before beginning discussion. Because poetry is usually more densely constructed than prose and highly selective in detail, it often lends itself to what we call *textual analysis*—looking closely at particular lines, words, and images as an entryway to discussing the whole work. Having readers share their different associations with a word or image can often help broaden interpretations.

DISCUSSING THE NOVELS

Many novels might come to mind that relate to the theme of the evil and the guilty. We have recommended *Coup de Grâce* and *Philadelphia Fire* as particularly enriching novels on this theme, and have provided interpretive questions that can be a significant aid to the reader. Even readers familiar with these novels will find a shared inquiry discussion of them a fresh and rewarding experience.

Most shared inquiry groups discuss a novel at a single discussion; some prefer to spread the discussion over more than one session, especially for longer novels. Since it is usually not realistic to expect participants to read a novel twice in full before discussion, we recommend that you at least reread parts of the novel that seemed especially important to you or that raised a number of questions in your mind. Our passages for textual analysis suggest parts of the novel where reading twice might be most valuable. You might even begin your discussion, after posing a basic question, by looking closely at one or two short passages to get people talking about central ideas and offering a variety of opinions that can be probed and expanded into a discussion of the whole work.

HOW THE GREAT BOOKS FOUNDATION CAN HELP YOU

The Great Books Foundation can be a significant resource for you and your discussion group. Our staff conducts shared inquiry workshops throughout the country that will help you or your entire group conduct better discussions. Thousands of people—from elementary school teachers and college professors to those who just love books and ideas—have found our workshops to be an enjoyable experience that changes forever how they approach literature.

The Foundation publishes a variety of reading series that might interest you. We invite you to call us at 1-800-222-5870 or visit our Web site at http://www.greatbooks.org. We can help you start a book group, put you in touch with established Great Books groups in your area, or give you information about many special events—such as poetry weekends or week-long discussion institutes—sponsored by Great Books groups around the country.

Finally, we invite you to inquire about Junior Great Books for students in kindergarten through high school, to learn how you can help develop the next generation of book lovers and shared inquiry participants.

We hope you enjoy *The Evil and the Guilty* and that it inaugurates many years of exciting discussions for your group. Great Books programs—for children as well as adults—are founded on the idea that readers discussing together can achieve insight and great pleasure from literature. We look forward, with you, to cultivating this idea through the next century.

Footnotes by the author are not bracketed; footnotes by
the Great Books Foundation, an editor,
or a translator are [bracketed].

AFTER THE BALL

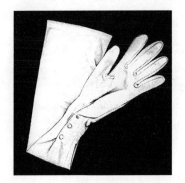

Leo Tolstoy

LEO TOLSTOY (1828–1910) was the son of
a Russian count and a princess. He inherited
his father's estate—and its 700 serfs—when he
was nineteen. After a youth of what he called
"vulgar licentiousness," including study, military
service, European travel, gadding about Moscow,
and writing acclaimed short stories, Tolstoy
returned to live on his estate. There he plunged
into social reforms, establishing a school for his
serfs and publishing a controversial magazine
about education. In 1869, Tolstoy's first major
novel, *War and Peace,* was published; *Anna
Karenina* followed in 1877. In the late 1870s,
a spiritual crisis led Tolstoy to embrace religion
and to practice—imperfectly—chastity and
vegetarianism. He translated the Gospels,
corresponded with Mahatma Gandhi, and
considered giving away his personal property
and entering a monastery. "Live seeking God
and then life will not exist without God,"
he wrote, yet also commented in his diary:
"Can't feel sorry for flies—there's a limit."
Tolstoy died at a railroad station after
mysteriously leaving home. During the last
moments of his life, he repeated over and over,
"I do not understand what it is I have to do."

S O YOU WOULD SAY that by himself a man cannot tell good from evil, that it's all a question of environment, that we are prey to our environment. But for my part I think it's all a matter of chance. Take my own case . . ."

This was how our highly respected friend, Ivan Vasilevich, began talking. We had been having a conversation to the effect that if ever the individual man were to be improved, one would have first of all to change the conditions in which people live. Now no one had actually said that it wasn't possible for a man by himself to tell good from evil, but Ivan Vasilevich had a way of responding to his own ideas as they were prompted by conversations and of using them as a pretext to relate episodes from his own life. Often, because he used to tell his story with such frankness and honesty, he would become quite engrossed in it and forget completely what had moved him to begin. This is what happened this time too.

"I'll tell you about my own case. My whole life was shaped the way it is, rather than any other, not by environment, but by something quite different."

"By what then?" we asked.

"Well, it's a long story. I'll need some time to make you understand."

"Go ahead, we're listening."

Ivan Vasilevich thought for a moment, then shook his head.

"Yes," he said. "From that one night, or rather that one morning onwards my whole life changed."

"So what happened then?"

"It happened that I was very much in love. I had fallen in love many times, but this was my greatest love. It's all over now; her daughters are already married. It was Varenka, yes, Varenka B." (Ivan Vasilevich gave her surname.) "Even at the age of fifty she was a remarkably beautiful woman. But in her youth, at eighteen, she was captivating: tall, slim, graceful, and regal, quite regal. She always carried herself extraordinarily erect, as if this were the only way possible for her, and her beauty and height, along with her habit of tilting her head back slightly, gave her an air of majesty, in spite of her thinness, or rather skinniness. This would have frightened people away from her, had it not been for the tender, invariably merry smile on her lips and in her brilliant, captivating eyes, and in the whole of her lovely young being."

"Just listen to how he describes her!"

"Yes, and however I describe her, I'll never be able to make you understand what she was like. But that doesn't matter. What I want to tell you about happened in the forties. At that time I was a student at a provincial university. I don't know whether it was a good thing or bad thing, but in our university at that time there were no philosophical circles and no theories, we were simply young, and we lived as young people do: we worked and we had a good time. I was a high-spirited and very lively young fellow, and rich into the bargain. I owned a fine thoroughbred, and I used to go tobogganing down the hills with the girls—skates were not yet in fashion; and I lived it up with my friends—we drank nothing but champagne at that time; if we didn't have any money, we drank nothing, but we didn't drink vodka like they do now. I enjoyed most of all going to soirées and balls. I could dance very well and was quite good-looking."

"Come now, there's no need to be modest," interrupted one of the women present. "We all know your picture, don't we? You were not just quite good-looking, you were very handsome."

"Handsome or not, that's not important. What is important, though, is that during the time my love for her was at its height, just before the beginning of Lent, I was at a ball given by the marshal of our province. He was a kindly old man, a generous host, and he held a position at court. His wife was equally kindly and, standing to receive her guests in a low-cut, brown velvet dress which left her plump, elderly white shoulders bare and wearing a diamond frontlet in her hair, she looked like portraits one sees of the Empress Elizabeth. The ball was wonderful. There was a splendid room where the musicians—the then highly acclaimed serf-orchestra of a local landowner-patron—had a gallery to themselves and where there was a magnificent buffet and an overflowing sea of champagne. Although I was a devotee of champagne, I didn't drink, because even without wine I was drunk with love, but to make up for it I danced until I was dropping—quadrilles, waltzes, and polkas—and of course as many of them as possible with Varenka. She was wearing a white dress with a pink sash, white kid gloves reaching almost to her thin pointed elbows, and white satin shoes. I was robbed of the mazurka: a quite repulsive engineer, Anisimov—I haven't yet been able to forgive him for what he did—had asked her for the dance as soon as she came into the room, whilst I had called in at my barber's for a pair of gloves and was late. So I didn't dance the mazurka with her, but with a German girl in whom I had taken some interest previously. But I fear on that evening I was very impolite to her,

I didn't talk to her and didn't look at her; I had eyes only for that tall, slim figure in the white dress with its pink sash, for Varenka's radiant, flushed face and her lovely tender eyes. Not only I, but everyone else was looking at her and admiring her, men and women alike, even though she put them all in the shade. It was impossible not to admire her.

"According to the rules, so to speak, I shouldn't have danced the mazurka with her, but in fact I danced with her almost the whole time. She would come boldly forward across the whole length of the room straight to me, and I would jump up without waiting for an invitation, and she would thank me with a smile for my quick-wittedness. Whenever our row was led up to hers, and she miscalculated my position in the set, she would give her hand to one of the other men, shrugging her thin little shoulders, and smile at me as a token of regret and consolation. Whenever there was a waltz figure in the mazurka, I waltzed with her for a long time. Breathing fast, she would smile and say 'Encore.' And I waltzed with her over and over again and could not feel my body."

"What do you mean, you couldn't feel it? When you put your arms around her waist I think you must have felt a lot, not only your own body, but hers too," said one of the guests.

Ivan Vasilevich suddenly blushed, and almost shouted in anger:

"Yes, that's just like you young people nowadays. You see nothing apart from a woman's body. It was not like that in our day. The more passionately I was in love, the less physical she became for me. Today you see legs, and ankles, and things like that, you undress the woman you love, for me, though, as Alphonse Karr said—and what a fine writer he was—the object of my love was always clad in bronze. Far from undressing those we love, we strove, like the good son of Noah, to cover up their nakedness. But you wouldn't understand any of that."

"Take no notice of him. Did anything happen after that?" one of us asked.

"Yes. So I went on dancing with her and didn't notice the time passing. The musicians struck up the same old mazurka tune over and over again with the sort of despairing weariness you often see at the end of a ball—you know the kind of thing—and in the drawing room the mamas and papas had already got up from their card tables ready for supper. The servants were more frequently hurrying through the room with various things. It was after two o'clock. I had to take advantage of these last minutes. I asked her to dance again, and for the hundredth time we glided down the room.

" 'So, is the quadrille after supper mine?' I said to her, taking her back to her place.

" 'Of course,' she said smiling, 'unless I have to go.'

" 'I won't let that happen,' I said.

" 'Give me my fan a moment,' she said.

" 'I'm reluctant to part with it,' I said, handing her the cheap little white fan.

" 'Well here you are then, so that you don't grieve,' she said, and she plucked a little feather from the fan and gave it to me. I took the feather, and only my eyes were able to express the rapturous gratitude I felt inside. I was not only cheerful and contented, I was happy, I was blissful, I was good, I was not myself, but some otherworldly being, ignorant of evil and capable only of good. I concealed the feather in my glove, and stood up, not having the strength to walk away from her.

" 'Look, they're asking papa to dance,' she said to me, pointing to the tall, imposing figure of her father, a colonel with silver epaulettes on his jacket, who was standing in the doorway with our hostess and some other women.

"The loud voice of our hostess with her diamond frontlet and her shoulders like the Empress Elizabeth's called over in our direction, 'Varenka, come here.' Varenka went over to the door, and I followed her. '*Ma chère,* do persuade your father to take the floor with you. Now please, Pyotr Vladislavich,' said our hostess, turning to the colonel.

7

"Varenka's father was a very handsome, elderly man, tall, stately, and well preserved. He had a ruddy face, a white upswept moustache à la Nicholas I, white whiskers which came to meet the moustache, and hair combed forward over his temples; and the same tender, merry smile as radiated from his daughter sparkled in his eyes and on his lips. He was superbly built, with a broad chest protruding in military fashion and modestly decorated with medals. His shoulders were strong and his legs long and slender. He was a military commander with the highly disciplined manner of an old campaigner under Nicholas.

"When we approached him the colonel tried to refuse, saying that he had forgotten how to dance, but eventually he smiled, swung his right arm to the left, and took his sword out of its sheath and handed it to an obliging young man standing nearby. Then, pulling a suede glove onto his right hand, he said with a smile, 'Everything according to the rules,' took his daughter's hand, and stood one quarter turned, waiting for the music.

"When the mazurka began he tapped one foot with gusto and struck out with the other, his tall, solid figure moving first of all gently, then noisily and spiritedly about the room, his soles stamping on the floor and his feet clicking together. Varenka's graceful figure glided beside him almost unnoticed as she shortened or lengthened the steps of her little white satin feet at just the right moment. The whole room followed their every movement. For myself I not only admired them, but felt an ecstatic tenderness as I watched them. I was especially moved by his boots with footstraps round them—they were fine calfskin boots, not the latest pointed type, but old-fashioned, with square toes and without heels. Obviously they had been made for him by the regimental cobbler. 'He doesn't buy fashionable boots, but wears homemade ones,' I thought. 'That's so he can bring his favorite daughter out in society and buy clothes for her.' And I found the square toes of his boots particularly touching. One could see that at one time he had been a superb dancer, but now he was heavy, and his legs had not sufficient spring for all those elegant and rapid steps he tried to execute. Nevertheless he still managed two circles round the room with agility. And on one occasion, when he quickly brought his legs together and—even though somewhat heavily—went down onto one knee, while she, smiling and straightening her skirt, glided smoothly around him, there was a loud burst of applause from everyone in the room. Raising himself with some effort, he gently and tenderly drew his daughter's face towards him and kissed her forehead, then he brought her over to me, thinking that I was dancing with her. I said that I was not her partner. 'Well, never mind, you dance with her now,' he said, smiling affectionately and replacing his sword in its sheath.

"Just as once one drop has been poured from a bottle its whole content bursts forth, in a great stream, so in my heart my love for Varenka released all that heart's latent capacity for love. At that moment I embraced the whole world with my love. I loved the hostess with her diamond frontlet and her Elizabethan neckline, and her husband and her guests and her servants and even Anisimov, the engineer, who was sulking because of me. And looking at her father, with his homemade boots and his tender smile—the same smile that Varenka had—I experienced an emotion of rapturous affection.

"The mazurka ended, and the hosts asked their guests in to supper, but Colonel B. declined, saying that he had to get up early next morning, and took his leave of the host and his wife. I was afraid he might take her away too, but she stayed with her mother.

"After supper I danced the promised quadrille with her and, even though I seemed to be infinitely happy, my happiness continued to grow. We said nothing of love. I asked neither her nor even myself whether she loved me. It was enough for me to love her. And I was afraid of only one thing—that something might spoil my happiness.

"When I arrived home, undressed, and began to think of sleep, I realized that that was quite impossible. In my hand I held the little feather from her fan and also one of her gloves which she had given me as she was leaving, when I had helped first her mother and then her into their carriage. I looked at these things, and without closing my eyes I could see her again before me. I saw her faced with a choice between two partners and trying to guess aright where I would be standing in the set; I saw her saying in her lovely voice, 'Pride? That's it, isn't it?' and joyfully giving me her hand; I saw her at supper lifting a glass of champagne to her lips and looking at me shyly with her soft eyes. But most vividly of all I saw her partnering her father, dancing smoothly round him and, with pride and delight for both her father and herself, looking at the admiring crowd around her. And I couldn't help uniting the two of them in a single overwhelming feeling of affection.

"At that time I was living with my late brother. In general my brother didn't like society and didn't go to balls, and now he was working for his examinations at the university and leading a highly proper life. He was asleep. I looked at his face, buried in the pillow and half-covered by a flannel blanket, and I felt lovingly sorry for him, sorry that he didn't know and couldn't share the happiness I was experiencing. Our servant Petrushka came to meet me with a candle and wanted to help me undress, but I sent him away. The sight of his sleepy face and his disheveled hair seemed to me intensely moving. Trying not to make a noise, I went on tiptoe to my room and sat down on the bed. No, I was too happy, I couldn't sleep. On top of that I was hot in our heated rooms and, without taking off my uniform, I crept quietly into the hall, put on my overcoat, opened the outside door, and went into the street.

"I had left the ball between four and five o'clock, then I had come home and sat there for a while, so that about two more hours had gone by, and when I went out it was already light. The weather was typical for that time of year. There was a fog, and slushy snow was melting on the paths and dripping from every roof. At that time Varenka's family was living at the far end of the town, just past a large open space, on one side of which there was a parade ground and on the other a girls' boarding school. I went along our deserted side street and out on to the main road, where pedestrians and carters with fire-wood on their sledges were beginning to appear. As the sledges moved, their runners grated against the surface of the road. The horses, rhythmically nodding their damp heads beneath their gleaming harnesses, and the draymen, splashing along in huge boots beside their carts, their shoulders covered with bast mats, and the houses along the road, which in the fog seemed to be towering above me—all these things I found especially pleasing and significant.

"As I came to the open space where their house stood, I could see at the other end of it, in the direction of the parade ground, some large black object, and from the same direction came the sound of pipe and drum. My heart still sang, and now and again I could still hear the tune of the mazurka. But this was some other kind of music, cruel and harsh. 'What on earth can that be?' I thought, and set off along the slippery path running through the middle of the open space in the direction of the noise. I had gone only a hundred yards or so when through the fog I was able to make out a large number of black figures. They were obviously soldiers. 'That's it, they're out training,' I thought and, together with a blacksmith in a short, greasy fur coat and an apron who was walking in front of me carrying something, I went closer. Soldiers in black uniforms were stand-ing in two lines opposite each other, all with their rifles at ease, and motionless. Behind them stood a drummer and a piper, incessantly playing the same shrill unpleasant tune. 'What's that they're doing?' I asked the blacksmith, who had stopped along-side me. 'They're making the Tatar run the gauntlet for trying to desert,' answered the blacksmith angrily, as he looked to the far end of the lines.

"I began to look in that direction too and caught sight of something terrible coming towards me between the two rows of soldiers. What was coming towards me was a man stripped to the waist and bound to the soldiers who were leading him for-ward. Alongside him was a tall officer in a greatcoat and a peaked cap, a figure who seemed familiar to me. With blows being showered upon him from both sides and dragging his feet through the slushy snow, the prisoner was moving towards me, his whole body twitching; sometimes he would fall backwards, whereupon the corporals who were leading him on with their rifles would push him forwards; and sometimes he would lurch forwards, whereupon they would pull him up and stop him falling over. And all the time the tall resolute officer strode firmly beside him. It was her father, with his ruddy face, white moustache, and whiskers.

"Every time he was hit the prisoner screwed up his face with pain and turned it, as if in surprise, to the side from which the blow came, and gritting his white teeth, he repeated over and over again the same words. Only when he drew quite close to me could I hear these words. He sobbed rather than spoke them: 'Brothers, have mercy; brothers, have mercy.' But his brothers had no mercy, and when the column drew level with me, I saw the soldier standing opposite me take a resolute step forward and, swishing his stick through the air, bring it down hard across the Tatar's back. The Tatar lurched forwards, but the corporals held him up, and a similar blow fell upon him from the other side, and then again from my side, and then again from the other side. The colonel strode alongside, looking now at his feet, now at the prisoner, inhaling deeply as he blew out his cheeks, and then slowly releasing the air through his pursed lips. Once the column had passed where I was standing I caught a glimpse through the ranks of the prisoner's back. It was something so bloody, so glaringly red and unreal, I couldn't believe it was the body of a man. 'Lord forgive them,' said the blacksmith alongside me out loud.

"The column disappeared into the distance, and all the time they continued to beat the stumbling, writhing man from both sides, and all the time the drum and the pipe went on playing, and the tall, imposing figure of the colonel strode with the same resolute step alongside the prisoner. Suddenly the colonel stopped and went quickly up to one of the soldiers. 'I'll teach you to be soft,' I heard his angry voice shout. 'So you're going to pat him like that, are you?' And I saw him with his strong, gloved fist punch a frightened, undersized, puny soldier in the face because he was not bringing his stick down hard enough on the red back of the Tatar. 'Bring fresh rods!' he shouted, looking round, and caught sight of me. Pretending he didn't know me, he turned away hastily, with a menacing, ill-tempered frown on his face. I was so ashamed I didn't know where to look; it was as if I had been caught committing the most despicable crime, and I lowered my eyes and hurried home. The roll of the drum and the whistling of the pipe rang in my ears the whole way, and I could hear the words, 'Brothers, have mercy,' and then the self-assured and angry voice of the colonel crying, 'So you're going to be soft with him, are you?' And in the meantime my heart had become so full with an almost physical anguish, bordering on nausea, that I stopped still several times, and it seemed as if my stomach were about to heave and purge itself of all the horror which had entered into me at that sight. I don't remember how I got home and into my bed. But, as soon as I started to fall asleep, I began to see and hear everything again and leapt up. 'Obviously he knows something that I don't,' I said to myself, thinking of the colonel. 'If I knew what he knows, I would understand what I saw and it wouldn't torment me.' But, however much I thought, I couldn't grasp what the colonel knew, and when eventually, towards evening, I fell asleep, it was only after I had visited a friend and drunk myself silly with him.

"Well, do you think I decided there and then that what I had seen was evil? Not at all. 'If it was done with such certainty, and was recognized by everyone as being inevitable, then it follows they must have known something I didn't,' I kept thinking, and tried to realize what that something was. But, hard as I tried, I couldn't understand. And without this understanding I was unable to go into the army, as I had wanted to do previously, and not only did I not serve as a soldier, I didn't take up a government position at all and, as you can see, I haven't made anything of my life."

"Oh, come, we know all about your not having made anything of your life," said one of us. "How many other people would have made nothing of their lives, if it hadn't been for you. That's what you really ought to say."

"Really! That's quite ridiculous," said Ivan Vasilevich with genuine annoyance.

"And what about your love?" we asked.

"Love? My love began to wane that very day. Whenever she fell into a thoughtful mood—and that used to happen quite a lot—a smile would appear on her face, and I would immediately recall the colonel on the parade ground and feel somehow awkward and uncomfortable; I stopped meeting her so often and my love just faded away. You see then what can happen, and how a man's entire life can be changed and redirected. And yet you say . . ." he concluded. ∽

INTERPRETIVE QUESTIONS
FOR DISCUSSION

Why does Ivan try to deny that what he saw on the parade ground was evil?

1. Why does Ivan understand the young people's discussion of improving the lot of the individual as a pronouncement that "by himself a man cannot tell good from evil"? (3)

2. Why does Ivan feel not himself, "but some otherworldly being, ignorant of evil and capable only of good" when Varenka gives him the feather from her cheap fan? (7)

3. Why, unlike Ivan, is the blacksmith able to condemn the beating of the Tatar?

4. Why is Ivan "so ashamed" when the colonel looks at him during the Tatar's punishment, as if he had been "caught committing the most despicable crime"? (13)

5. Why does the colonel pretend not to know Ivan when he sees him on the parade ground?

6. Why does Ivan say that the beating was done "with such certainty" and was recognized by everyone as being "inevitable" even though he sees the blacksmith and the puny soldier protesting it? (13)

7. Why does Ivan conclude that the colonel knows something that he doesn't?

8. Why does Ivan's experience at the parade ground keep him from taking up a profession and making anything of his life?

Suggested textual analysis
Pages 11–14: from "I began to look in that direction too," to the end of the story.

Why does Ivan's love for Varenka fade away after the ball?

1. Why does Ivan so vehemently declare that his love for Varenka was chaste and not in the least physical?

2. Why does Ivan stress Varenka's "majesty" and "regal" beauty as well as her "skinniness"? (4–6)

3. Why is it enough for Ivan that he loved Varenka, regardless of whether or not she loved him?

4. Why does Ivan feel an "ecstatic tenderness" as he watches Varenka and the colonel dance together? After the colonel tells Ivan to dance with his daughter, why does Ivan feel that all his heart's latent capacity for love was released and that he "embraced the whole world" with his love? (8–9)

5. Why isn't Ivan aware that his story portrays Varenka as a flirt and her father as a social climber?

6. Why does Varenka say to Ivan, "Pride? That's it, isn't it?" as she tries to guess where Ivan would be standing in the dance set? (10)

7. Why can't Ivan see Varenka without recalling her father on the parade ground? (14; cf. 10)

8. Why does Ivan need to be prompted by his listeners to finish the story of his love for Varenka?

Suggested textual analysis
Pages 6–7: beginning, "Yes, that's just like you young people nowadays," and ending, "not having the strength to walk away from her."

Is Ivan's refusal to join any service a sign of strength or of weakness—an indication of profound goodness or of a shallow and ineffectual character?

1. Why does Ivan believe that his whole life was shaped by his chance encounter with the colonel at the parade ground?

2. Why is Ivan proud of the way the fun-loving youth of his day behaved as compared with the more intellectual young people to whom he is speaking?

3. Do Ivan's young friends respect and admire him, or are they ridiculing him with their teasing?

4. Why does Ivan unselfconsciously depict himself as an irresponsible dandy who is keenly aware of distinctions in status and wealth?

5. Why, even though thirty years have passed, does Ivan say that he hasn't yet forgiven the repulsive engineer Anisimov for dancing the mazurka with Varenka?

6. Why does Tolstoy have Ivan's "highly proper" brother be asleep during and after the ball, and dead when Ivan tells his story? (10)

7. Why is Ivan genuinely annoyed at the suggestion that "many other people would have made nothing of their lives," if it hadn't been for him? (14)

8. Are we meant to think that Ivan's life was ruined by the incident at the parade ground?

Suggested textual analysis
Pages 8–10: beginning, "When the mazurka began," and ending, "in a single overwhelming feeling of affection."

FOR FURTHER REFLECTION

1. Can individuals "tell good from evil" on their own? Is our understanding of good and evil determined by our culture and "environment"?

2. Are people who witness evil without condemning it guilty of evil as well?

3. Can power exist without cruelty?

4. Can we live in a world where there is evil without compromising our own integrity?

5. Does the inability to face the dark side of life indicate a saintly or a cowardly nature?

ON EVIL, GUILT,
AND POWER

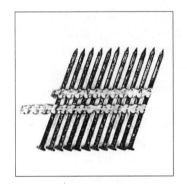

Friedrich Nietzsche

FRIEDRICH NIETZSCHE (1844–1900) studied classical philology at the universities of Bonn and Leipzig. He was such a prodigy that, at the age of twenty-four and without having completed his doctorate, he was awarded a professorship in classical philology at the University of Basel. What followed, however, was not the classical scholarship everyone had expected, but rather a series of works of radical philosophy whose influence on twentieth-century writers and thinkers has been profound. Nietzsche's style of philosophizing is unusual in that he does not try to develop a consistent philosophical system, even within a single work. Instead, he offers "aphorisms"—self-contained, carefully crafted meditations on a single theme that are conversational, witty, brilliant, and often mutually contradictory. Nietzsche suffered a mental breakdown in January 1889 and entered an asylum. He remained insane until the end of his life.

Our selection from Nietzsche's writings is taken from *Beyond Good and Evil, On the Genealogy of Morals,* and *The Will to Power.*

WE ARE UNKNOWN to ourselves, we men of knowledge—and with good reason. We have never sought ourselves—how could it happen that we should ever *find* ourselves? It has rightly been said: "Where your treasure is, there will your heart be also"; *our* treasure is where the beehives of our knowledge are. We are constantly making for them, being by nature winged creatures and honey-gatherers of the spirit; there is one thing alone we really care about from the heart—"bringing something home." Whatever else there is in life, so-called "experiences"—which of us has sufficient earnestness for them? Or sufficient time? Present experience has, I am afraid, always found us "absent-minded": we cannot give our hearts to it—not even our ears! Rather, as one divinely preoccupied and immersed in himself into whose ear the bell has just boomed with all its strength the twelve beats of noon suddenly starts up and asks himself, "What really was that which just struck?" so we sometimes rub our ears *afterward* and ask, utterly surprised and disconcerted, "What really was that which we have just experienced?" and moreover, "Who *are* we really?" and, afterward as aforesaid, count the twelve trembling bell-strokes of our experience, our life, our *being*—and alas! miscount them.—So we are necessarily strangers to ourselves, we do not comprehend ourselves, we *have* to misunderstand ourselves, for us the law "Each is furthest from himself" applies to all eternity—we are not "men of knowledge" with respect to ourselves.

Because of a scruple peculiar to me that I am loth to admit to— for it is concerned with *morality*, with all that has hitherto been celebrated on earth as morality—a scruple that entered my life so early, so uninvited, so irresistibly, so much in conflict with my environment, age, precedents, and descent that I might almost have the right to call it my "a priori"—my curiosity as well as my suspicions were bound to halt quite soon at the question of where our good and evil really *originated*. In fact, the problem of the origin of evil pursued me even as a boy of thirteen: at an age in which you have "half childish trifles, half God in your heart," I devoted to it my first childish literary trifle, my first philosophical effort—and as for the "solution" of the problem I posed at that time, well, I gave the honor to God, as was only fair, and made him the *father* of evil. . . .

Fortunately I learned early to separate theological prejudice from moral prejudice and ceased to look for the origin of evil *behind* the world. A certain amount of historical and philological schooling, together with an inborn fastidiousness of taste in respect to psychological questions in general, soon transformed my problem into another one: under what conditions did man devise these value judgments good and evil? *and what value do they themselves possess?* Have they hitherto hindered or furthered human prosperity? Are they a sign of distress, of impoverishment, of the degeneration of life? Or is there revealed in them, on the contrary, the plenitude, force, and will of life, its courage, certainty, future?

Thereupon I discovered and ventured divers answers; I distinguished between ages, peoples, degrees of rank among individuals; I departmentalized my problem; out of my answers there grew new questions, inquiries, conjectures, probabilities—until at length I had a country of my own, a soil of my own, an entire discrete, thriving, flourishing world, like a secret garden the existence of which no one suspected.—Oh how *fortunate* we are, we men of knowledge, provided only that we know how to keep silent long enough!

∽

Wandering through the many subtler and coarser moralities which have so far been prevalent on earth, or still are prevalent, I found that certain features recurred regularly together and were closely associated—until I finally discovered two basic types and one basic difference.

There are *master morality* and *slave morality*—I add immediately that in all the higher and more mixed cultures there also appear attempts at mediation between these two moralities, and yet more often the interpenetration and mutual misunderstanding of both, and at times they occur directly alongside each other—even in the same human being, within a *single* soul. The moral discrimination of values has originated either among a ruling group whose consciousness of its difference from the ruled group was accompanied by delight—or among the ruled, the slaves and dependents of every degree. . . .

The noble type of man experiences *itself* as determining values; it does not need approval; it judges, "what is harmful to me is harmful in itself"; it knows itself to be that which first accords honor to things; it is *value-creating*. Everything it knows as part of itself it honors: such a morality is self-glorification. In the foreground there is the feeling of fullness, of power that seeks to overflow, the happiness of high tension, the consciousness of wealth that would give and bestow: the noble human being, too, helps the unfortunate, but not, or almost not, from pity, but prompted more by an urge begotten by excess of power. The noble human being honors himself as one who is powerful, also as one who has power over himself, who knows how to speak and be silent, who delights in being severe and hard with himself and respects all severity and hardness. . . .

It is different with the second type of morality, *slave morality.* Suppose the violated, oppressed, suffering, unfree, who are uncertain of themselves and weary, moralize: what will their moral valuations have in common? Probably, a pessimistic suspicion about the whole condition of man will find expression, perhaps a condemnation of man along with his condition. The slave's eye is not favorable to the virtues of the powerful: he is skeptical and suspicious, *subtly* suspicious, of all the "good" that is honored there—he would like to persuade himself that even their happiness is not genuine. Conversely, those qualities are brought out and flooded with light which serve to ease existence for those who suffer: here pity, the complaisant and obliging hand, the warm heart, patience, industry, humility, and friendliness are honored—for here these are the most useful qualities and almost the only means for enduring the pressure of existence. Slave morality is essentially a morality of utility.

Here is the place for the origin of that famous opposition of "good" and "evil": into evil one's feelings project power and dangerousness, a certain terribleness, subtlety, and strength that does not permit contempt to develop. According to slave morality, those who are "evil" thus inspire fear; according to master morality it is precisely those who are "good" that inspire, and wish to inspire, fear, while the "bad" are felt to be contemptible.

∞

Now it is plain to me, . . . the judgment "good" did *not* originate with those to whom "goodness" was shown! Rather it was "the good" themselves, that is to say, the noble, powerful, high-stationed, and high-minded, who felt and established themselves and their actions as good, that is, of the first rank, in contradistinction to all the low, low-minded, common, and plebeian. It was out of this *pathos of distance* that they first seized the right to create values and to coin names for values: what had they to do with utility! The viewpoint of utility is as remote and inappropriate as it possibly could be in face of such a burning eruption of the highest rank-ordering, rank-defining value judgments: for here feeling has attained the antithesis of that low degree of warmth which any calculating prudence, any calculus of utility, presupposes—and not for once only, not for an exceptional hour, but for good. The pathos of nobility and distance, as aforesaid, the protracted and domineering fundamental total feeling on the part of a higher ruling order in relation to a lower order, to a "below"—*that* is the origin of the antithesis "good" and "bad." (The lordly right of giving names extends so far that one should allow oneself to conceive the origin of language itself as an expression of power on the part of the rulers: they say "this *is* this and this," they seal every thing and event with a sound and, as it were, take possession of it.) It follows from this origin that the word "good" was definitely *not* linked from the first and by necessity to "unegoistic" actions, as the superstition of these genealogists of morality would have it. Rather it was only when aristocratic value judgments *declined* that the whole antithesis "egoistic"/"unegoistic" obtruded itself more and more on the human conscience—it is, to speak in my own language, the *herd instinct* that through this antithesis at last gets its word (and its *words*) in. And even then it was a long time before that instinct attained such dominion that moral evaluation was actually stuck and halted at this antithesis (as, for example, is the case in contemporary Europe: the prejudice that takes "moral," "unegoistic," *"désintéressé"* as concepts of equivalent value already rules today with the force of a "fixed idea" and brain-sickness).

The signpost to the *right* road was for me the question: what was the real etymological significance of the designations for "good" coined in the various languages? I found they all led back to the *same conceptual transformation*—that everywhere "noble," "aristocratic" in the social sense, is the basic concept from which "good" in the sense of "with aristocratic soul," "noble," "with a soul of a high order," "with a privileged soul" necessarily developed: a development which always runs parallel with that other in which "common," "plebeian," "low" are finally transformed into the concept "bad."

⌒

Every enhancement of the type "man" has so far been the work of an aristocratic society—and it will be so again and again—a society that believes in the long ladder of an order of rank and differences in value between man and man, and that needs slavery in some sense or other. Without that *pathos of distance* which grows out of the ingrained difference between strata— when the ruling caste constantly looks afar and looks down upon subjects and instruments and just as constantly practices obedience and command, keeping down and keeping at a distance—that other, more mysterious pathos could not have grown up either—the craving for an ever new widening of distances within the soul itself, the development of ever higher, rarer, more remote, further-stretching, more comprehensive states—in brief, simply the enhancement of the type "man," the continual "self-overcoming of man," to use a moral formula in a supra-moral sense.

To be sure, one should not yield to humanitarian illusions about the origins of an aristocratic society (and thus of the presupposition of this enhancement of the type "man"): truth is hard. Let us admit to ourselves, without trying to be considerate, how every higher culture on earth so far has *begun*. Human beings whose nature was still natural, barbarians in every terrible sense of the word, men of prey who were still in possession of unbroken strength of will and lust for power, hurled themselves upon weaker, more civilized, more peaceful races, perhaps traders or cattle raisers, or upon mellow old cultures whose last vitality was even then flaring up in splendid fireworks of spirit and corruption. In the beginning, the noble caste was always the barbarian caste: their predominance did not lie mainly in physical strength but in strength of the soul—they were more *whole* human beings (which also means, at every level, "more whole beasts").

Refraining mutually from injury, violence, and exploitation and placing one's will on a par with that of someone else—this may become, in a certain rough sense, good manners among individuals if the appropriate conditions are present (namely, if these men are actually similar in strength and value standards and belong together in *one* body). But as soon as this principle is extended, and possibly even accepted as the *fundamental principle of society*, it immediately proves to be what it really is—a will to the *denial* of life, a principle of disintegration and decay.

Here we must beware of superficiality and get to the bottom of the matter, resisting all sentimental weakness: life itself is *essentially* appropriation, injury, overpowering of what is alien and weaker; suppression, hardness, imposition of one's own forms, incorporation, and at least, at its mildest, exploitation—but why should one always use those words in which a slanderous intent has been imprinted for ages?

Even the body within which individuals treat each other as equals, as suggested before—and this happens in every healthy aristocracy—if it is a living and not a dying body, has to do to other bodies what the individuals within it refrain from doing to each other: it will have to be an incarnate will to power, it will strive to grow, spread, seize, become predominant—not from any morality or immorality but because it is *living* and because life simply *is* will to power. But there is no point on which the ordinary consciousness of Europeans resists instruction as on this: everywhere people are now raving, even under scientific disguises, about coming conditions of society in which "the exploitative aspect" will be removed—which sounds to me as if they promised to invent a way of life that would dispense with all organic functions. "Exploitation" does not belong to a corrupt or imperfect and primitive society: it belongs to the *essence* of what lives, as a basic organic function; it is a consequence of the will to power, which is after all the will of life.

∽

The slave revolt in morality begins when *ressentiment* itself becomes creative and gives birth to values: the *ressentiment* of natures that are denied the true reaction, that of deeds, and compensate themselves with an imaginary revenge. While every noble morality develops from a triumphant affirmation of itself, slave morality from the outset says No to what is "outside," what is "different," what is "not itself"; and *this* No is its creative deed. This inversion of the value-positing eye—this *need* to direct one's view outward instead of back to oneself—is of the essence of *ressentiment:* in order to exist, slave morality always first needs a hostile external world; it needs, physiologically speaking, external stimuli in order to act at all—its action is fundamentally reaction.

The reverse is the case with the noble mode of valuation: it acts and grows spontaneously, it seeks its opposite only so as to affirm itself more gratefully and triumphantly—its negative concept "low," "common," "bad" is only a subsequently-invented pale, contrasting image in relation to its positive basic concept—filled with life and passion through and through—"we noble ones, we good, beautiful, happy ones!" When the noble mode of valuation blunders and sins against reality, it does so in respect to the sphere with which it is *not* sufficiently familiar, against a real knowledge of which it has indeed inflexibly guarded itself: in some circumstances it misunderstands the sphere it despises, that of the common man, of the lower orders; on the other hand, one should remember that, even supposing that the affect of contempt, of looking down from a superior height, *falsifies* the image of that which it despises, it will at any rate still be a much less serious falsification than that perpetrated on its opponent—*in effigie* of course—by the submerged hatred, the vengefulness of the impotent. There is indeed too much carelessness, too much taking lightly, too much looking away and impatience involved in contempt, even too much joyfulness, for it to be able to transform its object into a real caricature and monster. . . .

While the noble man lives in trust and openness with himself (*gennaios*[1] "of noble descent" underlines the nuance "upright" and probably also "naïve"), the man of *ressentiment* is neither upright nor naïve nor honest and straightforward with himself. His soul *squints;* his spirit loves hiding places, secret paths and back doors, everything covert entices him as *his* world, *his* security, *his* refreshment; he understands how to keep silent, how not to forget, how to wait, how to be provisionally self-deprecating and humble. A race of such men of *ressentiment* is bound to become eventually *cleverer* than any noble race; it will also honor cleverness to a far greater degree: namely, as a condition of existence of the first importance; while with noble men cleverness can easily acquire a subtle flavor of luxury and subtlety— for here it is far less essential than the perfect functioning of the regulating *unconscious* instincts or even than a certain imprudence, perhaps a bold recklessness whether in the face of danger or of the enemy, or that enthusiastic impulsiveness in anger, love, reverence, gratitude, and revenge by which noble souls have at all times recognized one another. *Ressentiment* itself, if it should appear in the noble man, consummates and exhausts itself in an immediate reaction, and therefore does not *poison:* on the other hand, it fails to appear at all on countless occasions on which it inevitably appears in the weak and impotent.

To be incapable of taking one's enemies, one's accidents, even one's misdeeds seriously for very long—that is the sign of strong, full natures in whom there is an excess of the power to form, to mold, to recuperate, and to forget. . . . Such a man shakes off with a *single* shrug many vermin that eat deep into others; here alone genuine "love of one's enemies" is possible—

---

1. [High-born, noble, high-minded. —TRANS.]

supposing it to be possible at all on earth. How much reverence has a noble man for his enemies!—and such reverence is a bridge to love.—For he desires his enemy for himself, as his mark of distinction; he can endure no other enemy than one in whom there is nothing to despise and *very much* to honor! In contrast to this, picture "the enemy" as the man of *ressentiment* conceives him—and here precisely is his deed, his creation: he has conceived "the evil enemy," "*the Evil One,*" and this in fact is his basic concept, from which he then evolves, as an after-thought and pendant, a "good one"—himself!

This, then, is quite the contrary of what the noble man does, who conceives the basic concept "good" in advance and spon-taneously out of himself and only then creates for himself an idea of "bad"! This "bad" of noble origin and that "evil" out of the cauldron of unsatisfied hatred—the former an after-production, a side issue, a contrasting shade, the latter on the contrary the original thing, the beginning, the distinctive *deed* in the conception of a slave morality—how different these words "bad" and "evil" are, although they are both apparently the opposite of the same concept "good." But it is *not* the same con-cept "good": one should ask rather precisely *who* is "evil" in the sense of the morality of *ressentiment*. The answer, in all strictness, is: *precisely* the "good man" of the other morality, pre-cisely the noble, powerful man, the ruler, but dyed in another color, interpreted in another fashion, seen in another way by the venomous eye of *ressentiment.*

Here there is one thing we shall be the last to deny: he who knows these "good men" only as enemies knows only *evil ene-mies,* and the same men who are held so sternly in check *inter pares*[2] by custom, respect, usage, gratitude, and even more by mutual suspicion and jealousy, and who on the other hand in their relations with one another show themselves so resource-ful in consideration, self-control, delicacy, loyalty, pride, and friendship—once they go outside, where the strange, the

2. [Among equals. —TRANS.]

stranger is found, they are not much better than uncaged beasts of prey. There they savor a freedom from all social constraints, they compensate themselves in the wilderness for the tension engendered by protracted confinement and enclosure within the peace of society, they go *back* to the innocent conscience of the beast of prey, as triumphant monsters who perhaps emerge from a disgusting procession of murder, arson, rape, and torture, exhilarated and undisturbed of soul, as if it were no more than a students' prank, convinced they have provided the poets with a lot more material for song and praise. One cannot fail to see at the bottom of all these noble races the beast of prey, the splendid *blond beast* prowling about avidly in search of spoil and victory; this hidden core needs to erupt from time to time, the animal has to get out again and go back to the wilderness: the Roman, Arabian, Germanic, Japanese nobility, the Homeric heroes, the Scandinavian Vikings—they all shared this need. . . .

Supposing that what is at any rate believed to be the "truth" really is true, and the *meaning of all culture* is the reduction of the beast of prey "man" to a tame and civilized animal, a *domestic animal,* then one would undoubtedly have to regard all those instincts of reaction and *ressentiment* through whose aid the noble races and their ideals were finally confounded and overthrown as the actual *instruments of culture;* which is not to say that the *bearers* of these instincts themselves represent culture. Rather is the reverse not merely probable—no! today it is *palpable*! These bearers of the oppressive instincts that thirst for reprisal, the descendants of every kind of European and non-European slavery, and especially of the entire pre-Aryan populace—they represent the *regression* of mankind! These "instruments of culture" are a disgrace to man and rather an accusation and counterargument against "culture" in general! One may be quite justified in continuing to fear the blond beast at the core of all noble races and in being on one's guard against it: but who would not a hundred times sooner fear where one can also admire than *not* fear but be permanently condemned to the repellent sight of the ill-constituted, dwarfed, atrophied, and poisoned? And is that not *our* fate? What today constitutes *our* antipathy to "man"?—for we *suffer* from man, beyond doubt.

Dislike "taste"

Not fear; rather that we no longer have anything left to fear in man; that the maggot "man" is swarming in the foreground; that the "tame man," the hopelessly mediocre and insipid man, has already learned to feel himself as the goal and zenith, as the meaning of history, as "higher man"—that he has indeed a certain right to feel thus, insofar as he feels himself elevated above the surfeit of ill-constituted, sickly, weary, and exhausted people of which Europe is beginning to stink today, as something at least relatively well-constituted, at least still capable of living, at least affirming life.

At this point I cannot suppress a sigh and a last hope. What is it that I especially find utterly unendurable? That I cannot cope with, that makes me choke and faint? Bad air! Bad air! The approach of some ill-constituted thing; that I have to smell the entrails of some ill-constituted soul!

How much one is able to endure: distress, want, bad weather, sickness, toil, solitude. Fundamentally one can cope with everything else, born as one is to a subterranean life of struggle; one emerges again and again into the light, one experiences again and again one's golden hour of victory—and then one stands forth as one was born, unbreakable, tensed, ready for new, even harder, remoter things, like a bow that distress only serves to draw tauter.

But grant me from time to time—if there are divine goddesses in the realm beyond good and evil—grant me the sight, but *one* glance of something perfect, wholly achieved, happy, mighty, triumphant, something still capable of arousing fear! Of a man who justifies *man,* of a complementary and redeeming lucky hit on the part of man for the sake of which one may still *believe in man*!

For this is how things are: the diminution and leveling of European man constitutes *our* greatest danger, for the sight of him makes us weary.—We can see nothing today that wants to grow greater, we suspect that things will continue to go down, down, to become thinner, more good-natured, more prudent, more comfortable, more mediocre, more indifferent, more Chinese, more Christian—there is no doubt that man is getting "better" all the time.

Here precisely is what has become a fatality for Europe—together with the fear of man we have also lost our love of him, our reverence for him, our hopes for him, even the will to him. The sight of man now makes us weary—what is nihilism today if it is not *that?*—We are weary *of man.*

But let us return: the problem of the *other* origin of the "good," of the good as conceived by the man of *ressentiment,* demands its solution.

That lambs dislike great birds of prey does not seem strange: only it gives no ground for reproaching these birds of prey for bearing off little lambs. And if the lambs say among themselves, "These birds of prey are evil; and whoever is least like a bird of prey, but rather its opposite, a lamb—would he not be good?" there is no reason to find fault with this institution of an ideal, except perhaps that the birds of prey might view it a little ironically and say, "*We* don't dislike them at all, these good little lambs; we even love them: nothing is more tasty than a tender lamb."

To demand of strength that it should *not* express itself as strength, that it should *not* be a desire to overcome, a desire to throw down, a desire to become master, a thirst for enemies and resistances and triumphs, is just as absurd as to demand of weakness that it should express itself as strength. A quantum of force is equivalent to a quantum of drive, will, effect—more, it is nothing other than precisely this very driving, willing, effecting, and only owing to the seduction of language (and of the fundamental errors of reason that are petrified in it) which conceives and misconceives all effects as conditioned by something that causes effects, by a "subject," can it appear otherwise. For just as the popular mind separates the lightning from its flash and takes the latter for an *action,* for the operation of a subject called lightning, so popular morality also separates strength from expressions of strength, as if there were a neutral substratum behind the strong man, which was *free* to express strength or not to do so. But there is no such substratum; there is no "being" behind doing, effecting, becoming; "the doer" is merely a fiction added to the deed—the deed is everything. The popular mind in fact doubles the deed; when it sees the lightning flash, it is the deed of a deed: it posits the same event first as cause and then a second time as its effect. . . . [N]o wonder if the submerged, darkly glowering emotions of vengefulness and hatred exploit this belief for their own ends and in fact maintain no belief more ardently than the belief that *the strong man is free* to be weak and the bird of prey to be a lamb—for thus they gain the right to make the bird of prey *accountable* for being a bird of prey.

When the oppressed, downtrodden, outraged exhort one another with the vengeful cunning of impotence: "let us be different from the evil, namely good! And he is good who does not outrage, who harms nobody, who does not attack, who does not requite, who leaves revenge to God, who keeps himself hidden as we do, who avoids evil and desires little from life, like us, the patient, humble, and just"—this, listened to calmly and without previous bias, really amounts to no more than: "we weak ones are, after all, weak; it would be good if we did nothing *for which we are not strong enough*"; but this dry matter of fact, this prudence of the lowest order which even insects possess (posing as dead, when in great danger, so as not to do "too much"), has, thanks to the counterfeit and self-deception of impotence, clad itself in the ostentatious garb of the virtue of quiet, calm resignation, just as if the weakness of the weak—that is to say, their *essence,* their effects, their sole ineluctable, irremovable reality—were a voluntary achievement, willed, chosen, a *deed,* a *meritorious* act. This type of man *needs* to believe in a neutral independent "subject," prompted by an instinct for self-preservation and self-affirmation in which every lie is sanctified. The subject (or, to use a more popular expression, the *soul*) has perhaps been believed in hitherto more firmly than anything else on earth because it makes possible to the majority of mortals, the weak and oppressed of every kind, the sublime self-deception that interprets weakness as freedom, and their being thus-and-thus as a *merit*.

But how did that other "somber thing," the consciousness of guilt, the "bad conscience," come into the world?—And at this point we return to the genealogists of morals. To say it again— or haven't I said it yet?—they are worthless. A brief span of experience that is merely one's own, merely modern; no knowledge or will to knowledge of the past; even less of historical instinct, of that "second sight" needed here above all—and yet they undertake history of morality: it stands to reason that their results stay at a more than respectful distance from the truth. Have these genealogists of morals had even the remotest suspicion that, for example, the major moral concept *Schuld* [guilt] has its origin in the very material concept *Schulden* [debts]?[3] Or that punishment, as requital, evolved quite independently of any presupposition concerning freedom or nonfreedom of the will?—to such an extent, indeed, that a *high* degree of humanity had to be attained before the animal "man" began even to make the much more primitive distinctions between "intentional," "negligent," "accidental," "accountable," and their opposites and to take them into account when determining punishments. The idea, now so obvious, apparently so natural, even unavoidable, that had to serve as the explanation of how the sense of

---

3. [The German equivalent of "guilt" is *Schuld,* and the German for "debt(s)" is *Schuld(en).* "Innocent" is *unschuldig,* "debtor" is *Schuldner,* and so forth. This obviously poses problems for an English translation of this essay, but once the point has been clearly stated, no misunderstandings need result. Nietzsche's claims obviously do not *depend* on the double meaning of a German word, nor are they weakened by the fact that in English there are two different words, one derived from an Anglo-Saxon root, the other from Latin. —TRANS.]

justice ever appeared on earth—"the criminal deserves punishment *because* he could have acted differently"—is in fact an extremely late and subtle form of human judgment and inference: whoever transposes it to the beginning is guilty of a crude misunderstanding of the psychology of more primitive mankind. Throughout the greater part of human history punishment was *not* imposed *because* one held the wrongdoer responsible for his deed, thus *not* on the presupposition that only the guilty one should be punished: rather, as parents still punish their children, from anger at some harm or injury, vented on the one who caused it—but this anger is held in check and modified by the idea that every injury has its *equivalent* and can actually be paid back, even if only through the *pain* of the culprit. And whence did this primeval, deeply rooted, perhaps by now ineradicable idea draw its power—this idea of an equivalence between injury and pain? I have already divulged it: in the contractual relationship between *creditor* and *debtor,* which is as old as the idea of "legal subjects" and in turn points back to the fundamental forms of buying, selling, barter, trade, and traffic.

It was in *this* sphere then, the sphere of legal obligations, that the moral conceptual world of "guilt," "conscience," "duty," "sacredness of duty" had its origin: its beginnings were, like the beginnings of everything great on earth, soaked in blood thoroughly and for a long time. And might one not add that, fundamentally, this world has never since lost a certain odor of blood and torture? (Not even in good old Kant: the categorical imperative smells of cruelty.) It was here, too, that that uncanny intertwining of the ideas "guilt and suffering" was first effected—and by now they may well be inseparable. To ask it again: to what extent can suffering balance debts or guilt? To the extent that to *make* suffer was in the highest degree pleasurable, to the extent that the injured party exchanged for the loss he had sustained, including the displeasure caused by the loss, an extraordinary counterbalancing pleasure: that of *making* suffer—a genuine *festival,* something which, as aforesaid, was prized the more highly the more violently it contrasted with the rank and social standing of the creditor. This is offered only as a conjecture; for the depths of such subterranean things are difficult to fathom, besides being painful; and whoever clumsily interposes the concept of "revenge" does not enhance his insight into the matter but further veils and darkens it (for revenge merely leads us back to the same problem: "how can making suffer constitute a compensation?").

It seems to me that the delicacy and even more the tartuffery of tame domestic animals (which is to say modern men, which is to say us) resists a really vivid comprehension of the degree to which *cruelty* constituted the great festival pleasure of more primitive men and was indeed an ingredient of almost every one of their pleasures; and how naïvely, how innocently their thirst for cruelty manifested itself, how, as a matter of principle, they posited "disinterested malice" (or, in Spinoza's words, *sympathia malevolens*) as a *normal* quality of man—and thus as something to which the conscience cordially says *Yes!* A more profound eye might perceive enough of this oldest and most fundamental festival pleasure of man even in our time. . . . In any event, it is not long since princely weddings and public festivals of the more magnificent kind were unthinkable without executions, torturings, or perhaps an auto-da-fé, and no noble household was without creatures upon whom one could heedlessly vent one's malice and cruel jokes. (Consider, for instance, Don Quixote at the court of the Duchess. Today we read *Don Quixote* with a bitter taste in our mouths, almost with a feeling of torment, and would thus seem very strange and incomprehensible to its author and his contemporaries: they read it with the clearest conscience in the world as the most cheerful of books, they laughed themselves almost to death over it.) To see others suffer does one good, to make others suffer even more: this is a hard saying but an ancient, mighty, human, all-too-human principle to which even the apes might subscribe; for it has been said that in devising bizarre cruelties they anticipate man and are, as it were, his "prelude." Without cruelty there is no festival: thus the longest and most ancient part of human history teaches—and in punishment there is so much that is *festive!*

With this idea, by the way, I am by no means concerned to furnish our pessimists with more grist for their discordant and creaking mills of life-satiety. On the contrary, let me declare expressly that in the days when mankind was not yet ashamed of its cruelty, life on earth was more cheerful than it is now that pessimists exist. The darkening of the sky above mankind has deepened in step with the increase in man's feeling of shame *at man*. The weary pessimistic glance, mistrust of the riddle of life, the icy No of disgust with life—these do not characterize the most *evil* epochs of the human race: rather do they first step into the light of day as the swamp weeds they are when the swamp to which they belong comes into being—I mean the morbid softening and moralization through which the animal "man" finally learns to be ashamed of all his instincts. On his way to becoming an "angel" (to employ no uglier word) man has evolved that queasy stomach and coated tongue through which not only the joy and innocence of the animal but life itself has become repugnant to him—so that he sometimes holds his nose in his own presence and, with Pope Innocent the Third, disapprovingly catalogues his own repellent aspects ("impure begetting, disgusting means of nutrition in his mother's womb, baseness of the matter out of which man evolves, hideous stink, secretion of saliva, urine, and filth").

Today, when suffering is always brought forward as the principal argument *against* existence, as the worst question mark, one does well to recall the ages in which the opposite opinion prevailed because men were unwilling to refrain from *making* suffer and saw in it an enchantment of the first order, a genuine seduction *to* life. Perhaps in those days—the delicate may be comforted by this thought—pain did not hurt as much as it does now; at least that is the conclusion a doctor may arrive at who has treated Negroes (taken as representatives of prehistoric man) for severe internal inflammations that would drive even

Maybe they learned this to survive

the best-constituted European to distraction—in the case of
Negroes they do *not* do so. (The curve of human susceptibility
to pain seems in fact to take an extraordinary and almost sudden drop as soon as one has passed the upper ten thousand or *what*
ten million of the top stratum of culture; and for my own part,
I have no doubt that the combined suffering of all the animals
ever subjected to the knife for scientific ends is utterly negligible
compared with *one* painful night of a single hysterical blue-
stocking.) Perhaps the possibility may even be allowed that this
joy in cruelty does not really have to have died out: if pain hurts
more today, it simply requires a certain sublimation and sub-
tilization, that is to say it has to appear translated into the imaginative and psychical and adorned with such innocent names
that even the tenderest and most hypocritical conscience is not
suspicious of them ("tragic pity" is one such name; *les nostal-
gies de la croix*[4] is another).

What really arouses indignation against suffering is not suffering as such but the senselessness of suffering: but neither for
the Christian, who has interpreted a whole mysterious machin-
ery of salvation into suffering, nor for the naïve man of more
ancient times, who understood all suffering in relation to the
spectator of it or the causer of it, was there any such thing as
senseless suffering. So as to abolish hidden, undetected, unwit-
nessed suffering from the world and honestly to deny it, one was
in the past virtually compelled to invent gods and genii of all the
heights and depths, in short something that roams even in
secret, hidden places, sees even in the dark, and will not easily
let an interesting painful spectacle pass unnoticed. For it was
with the aid of such inventions that life then knew how to work
the trick which it has always known how to work, that of justifying itself, of justifying its "evil." Nowadays it might require
other auxiliary inventions (for example, life as a riddle, life as
an epistemological problem). "Every evil the sight of which edi-
fies a god is justified": thus spoke the primitive logic of feeling—

---

4. [The nostalgia of the cross. —TRANS.]

and was it, indeed, only primitive? The gods conceived of as the friends of *cruel* spectacles—oh how profoundly this ancient idea still permeates our European humanity! Merely consult Calvin and Luther. It is certain, at any rate, that the *Greeks* still knew of no tastier spice to offer their gods to season their happiness than the pleasures of cruelty. With what eyes do you think Homer made his gods look down upon the destinies of men? What was at bottom the ultimate meaning of Trojan Wars and other such tragic terrors? There can be no doubt whatever: they were intended as *festival plays* for the gods; and, insofar as the poet is in these matters of a more "godlike" disposition than other men, no doubt also as festival plays for the poets.

It was in the same way that the moral philosophers of Greece later imagined the eyes of God looking down upon the moral struggle, upon the heroism and self-torture of the virtuous: the "Herakles of duty" was on a stage and knew himself to be; virtue without a witness was something unthinkable for this nation of actors. Surely, that philosophers' invention, so bold and so fateful, which was then first devised for Europe, the invention of "free will," of the absolute spontaneity of man in good and in evil, was devised above all to furnish a right to the idea that the interest of the gods in man, in human virtue, *could never be exhausted.* There must never be any lack of real novelty, of really unprecedented tensions, complications, and catastrophies on the stage of the earth: the course of a completely deterministic world would have been predictable for the gods and they would have quickly grown weary of it—reason enough for those *friends of the gods,* the philosophers, not to inflict such a deterministic world on their gods! The entire mankind of antiquity is full of tender regard for "the spectator," as an essentially public, essentially visible world which cannot imagine happiness apart from spectacles and festivals.—And, as aforesaid, even in great *punishment* there is so much that is festive!

At this point I can no longer avoid giving a first, provisional statement of my own hypothesis concerning the origin of the "bad conscience": it may sound rather strange and needs to be pondered, lived with, and slept on for a long time. I regard the bad conscience as the serious illness that man was bound to contract under the stress of the most fundamental change he ever experienced—that change which occurred when he found himself finally enclosed within the walls of society and of peace. The situation that faced sea animals when they were compelled to become land animals or perish was the same as that which faced these semi-animals, well adapted to the wilderness, to war, to prowling, to adventure: suddenly all their instincts were disvalued and "suspended." From now on they had to walk on their feet and "bear themselves" whereas hitherto they had been borne by the water: a dreadful heaviness lay upon them. They felt unable to cope with the simplest undertakings; in this new world they no longer possessed their former guides, their regulating, unconscious, and infallible drives: they were reduced to thinking, inferring, reckoning, coordinating cause and effect, these unfortunate creatures; they were reduced to their "consciousness," their weakest and most fallible organ! I believe there has never been such a feeling of misery on earth, such a leaden discomfort—and at the same time the old instincts had not suddenly ceased to make their usual demands! Only it was hardly or rarely possible to humor them: as a rule they had to seek new and, as it were, subterranean gratifications.

All instincts that do not discharge themselves outwardly *turn inward*—this is what I call the *internalization* of man: thus it was that man first developed what was later called his "soul." The entire inner world, originally as thin as if it were stretched between two membranes, expanded and extended itself, acquired depth, breadth, and height, in the same measure as outward discharge was *inhibited*. Those fearful bulwarks with which the political organization protected itself against the old instincts of freedom—punishments belong among these bulwarks—brought about that all those instincts of wild, free, prowling man turned backward *against man himself*. Hostility, cruelty, joy in persecuting, in attacking, in change, in destruction—all this turned against the possessors of such instincts: *that* is the origin of the "bad conscience."

The man who, from lack of external enemies and resistances and forcibly confined to the oppressive narrowness and punctiliousness of custom, impatiently lacerated, persecuted, gnawed at, assaulted, and maltreated himself; this animal that rubbed itself raw against the bars of its cage as one tried to "tame" it; this deprived creature, racked with homesickness for the wild, who had to turn himself into an adventure, a torture chamber, an uncertain and dangerous wilderness—this fool, this yearning and desperate prisoner, became the inventor of the "bad conscience." But thus began the gravest and uncanniest illness, from which humanity has not yet recovered, man's suffering *of man, of himself*—the result of a forcible sundering from his animal past, as it were, a leap and plunge into new surroundings and conditions of existence, a declaration of war against the old instincts upon which his strength, joy, and terribleness had rested hitherto.

Let us add at once that, on the other hand, the existence on earth of an animal soul turned against itself, taking sides against itself, was something so new, profound, unheard of, enigmatic, contradictory, *and pregnant with a future* that the aspect of the earth was essentially altered. Indeed, divine spectators were needed to do justice to the spectacle that thus began and the end of which is not yet in sight—a spectacle too subtle, too marvelous, too paradoxical to be played senselessly unobserved on some ludicrous planet! From now on, man is *included* among the most unexpected and exciting lucky throws in the dice game of Heraclitus' "great child," be he called Zeus or chance; he gives rise to an interest, a tension, a hope, almost a certainty, as if with him something were announcing and preparing itself, as if man were not a goal but only a way, an episode, a bridge, a great promise.—

Among the presuppositions of this hypothesis concerning the origin of the bad conscience is, first, that the change referred to was not a gradual or voluntary one and did not represent an organic adaptation to new conditions but a break, a leap, a compulsion, an ineluctable disaster which precluded all struggle and even all *ressentiment*. Secondly, however, that the welding of a hitherto unchecked and shapeless populace into a firm form was not only instituted by an act of violence but also carried to its conclusion by nothing but acts of violence—that the oldest "state" thus appeared as a fearful tyranny, as an oppressive and remorseless machine, and went on working until this raw material of people and semi-animals was at last not only thoroughly kneaded and pliant but also *formed*.

I employed the word "state": it is obvious what is meant—some pack of blond beasts of prey, a conqueror and master race which, organized for war and with the ability to organize, unhesitatingly lays its terrible claws upon a populace perhaps tremendously superior in numbers but still formless and nomad. That is after all how the "state" began on earth: I think that sentimentalism which would have it begin with a "contract" has been disposed of. He who can command, he who is by nature "master," he who is violent in act and bearing—what has he to do with contracts! One does not reckon with such natures; they come like fate, without reason, consideration, or pretext; they appear as lightning appears, too terrible, too sudden, too convincing, too "different" even to be hated. Their work is an instinctive creation and imposition of forms; they are the most involuntary, unconscious artists there are—wherever they appear something new soon arises, a ruling structure that *lives*, in which parts and functions are delimited and coordinated, in which nothing whatever finds a place that has not first been assigned a "meaning" in relation to the whole. They do not know what guilt, responsibility, or consideration are, these born organizers; they exemplify that terrible artists' egoism that has the look of bronze and knows itself justified to all eternity in its "work," like a mother in her child. It is not in *them* that the "bad conscience" developed, that goes without saying—but it would not have developed *without them*, this ugly growth, it would be lacking if a tremendous quantity of freedom had not been expelled from the world, or at least from the visible world, and made as it were *latent* under their hammer blows and artists' violence. This *instinct for freedom* forcibly made latent—we have seen it already—this instinct for freedom pushed back and repressed, incarcerated within and finally able to discharge and vent itself only on itself: that, and that alone, is what the *bad conscience* is in its beginnings.

One should guard against thinking lightly of this phenomenon merely on account of its initial painfulness and ugliness. For fundamentally it is the same active force that is at work on a grander scale in those artists of violence and organizers who build states, and that here, internally, on a smaller and pettier scale, directed backward, in the "labyrinth of the breast," to use Goethe's expression, creates for itself a bad conscience and builds negative ideals—namely, the *instinct for freedom* (in my language: the will to power); only here the material upon which the form-giving and ravishing nature of this force vents itself is man himself, his whole ancient animal self—and *not,* as in that greater and more obvious phenomenon, some *other* man, *other* men. This secret self-ravishment, this artists' cruelty, this delight in imposing a form upon oneself as a hard, recalcitrant, suffering material and in burning a will, a critique, a contradiction, a contempt, a No into it, this uncanny, dreadfully joyous labor of a soul voluntarily at odds with itself that makes itself suffer out of joy in making suffer—eventually this entire *active* "bad conscience"—you will have guessed it—as the womb of all ideal and imaginative phenomena, also brought to light an abundance of strange new beauty and affirmation, and perhaps beauty itself.—After all, what would be "beautiful" if the contradiction had not first become conscious of itself, if the ugly had not first said to itself, "I am ugly"?

This hint will at least make less enigmatic the enigma of how contradictory concepts such as *selflessness, self-denial, self-sacrifice* can suggest an ideal, a kind of beauty; and one thing we know henceforth—I have no doubt of it—and that is the nature of the *delight* that the selfless man, the self-denier, the self-sacrificer feels from the first: this delight is tied to cruelty.

So much for the present about the origin of the moral value of the "unegoistic," about the soil from which this value grew: only the bad conscience, only the will to self-maltreatment provided the conditions for the *value* of the unegoistic.—

The bad conscience is an illness, there is no doubt about that, but an illness as pregnancy is an illness. Let us seek out the conditions under which this illness has reached its most terrible and most sublime height; we shall see what it really was that thus entered the world. But for that one needs endurance—and first of all we must go back again to an earlier point of view.

The civil-law relationship between the debtor and his creditor, discussed above, has been interpreted in an, historically speaking, exceedingly remarkable and dubious manner into a relationship in which to us modern men it seems perhaps least to belong: namely into the relationship between the present generation and its ancestors.

Within the original tribal community—we are speaking of primeval times—the living generation always recognized a juridical duty toward earlier generations, and especially toward the earliest, which founded the tribe (and by no means a merely sentimental obligation: there are actually reasons for denying the existence of the latter for the greater part of human history). The conviction reigns that it is only through the sacrifices and accomplishments of the ancestors that the tribe *exists*—and that one has to *pay them back* with sacrifices and accomplishments: one thus recognizes a *debt* that constantly grows greater, since these forebears never cease, in their continued existence as powerful spirits, to accord the tribe new advantages and new strength. In vain, perhaps? But there is no "in vain" for these rude and "poor-souled" ages. What can one give them in return? Sacrifices (initially as food in the coarsest sense), feasts, music, honors; above all, obedience—for all customs, as works of the ancestors, are also their statutes and commands: can one ever give them enough? This suspicion remains and increases; from time to time it leads to a wholesale sacrifice, something tremendous in the way of repayment to the "creditor" (the notorious sacrifice of the first-born, for example; in any case blood, human blood).

The *fear* of the ancestor and his power, the consciousness of indebtedness to him, increases, according to this kind of logic, in exactly the same measure as the power of the tribe itself increases, as the tribe itself grows ever more victorious, independent, honored, and feared. By no means the other way round! Every step toward the decline of a tribe, every misfortune, every sign of degeneration, of coming disintegration always *diminishes* fear of the spirit of its founder and produces a meaner impression of his cunning, foresight, and present power. If one imagines this rude kind of logic carried to its end, then the ancestors of the *most powerful* tribes are bound eventually to grow to monstrous dimensions through the imagination of growing fear and to recede into the darkness of the divinely uncanny and unimaginable: in the end the ancestor must necessarily be transfigured into a *god*. Perhaps this is even the origin of gods, an origin therefore out of *fear!* . . . And whoever should feel obliged to add, "but out of piety also!" would hardly be right for the greater part of the existence of man, his prehistory. To be sure, he would be quite right for the *intermediate* age, in which the noble tribes developed—who indeed paid back their originators, their ancestors (heroes, gods) with interest all the qualities that had become palpable in themselves, the *noble* qualities. We shall take another look later at the ennoblement of the gods (which should not be confused with their becoming "holy"); let us first of all follow to its end the course of this whole development of the consciousness of guilt.

History shows that the consciousness of being in debt to the deity did not by any means come to an end together with the organization of communities on the basis of blood relationship. Even as mankind inherited the concepts "good" and "bad" from the tribal nobility (along with its basic psychological propensity to set up orders of rank), it also inherited, along with the tribal and family divinities, the burden of still unpaid debts and of the desire to be relieved of them. (The transition is provided by those numerous slave and dependent populations who, whether through compulsion or through servility and mimicry, adapted themselves to their masters' cult of the gods: this inheritance then overflows from them in all directions.) The guilty feeling of indebtedness to the divinity continued to grow for several millennia—always in the same measure as the concept of God and the feeling for divinity increased on earth and was carried to the heights. (The entire history of ethnic struggle, victory, reconciliation, fusion, everything that precedes the definitive ordering of rank of the different national elements in every great racial synthesis, is reflected in the confused genealogies of their gods, in the sagas of the gods' struggles, victories, and reconciliations; the advance toward universal empires is always also an advance toward universal divinities; despotism with its triumph over the independent nobility always prepares the way for some kind of monotheism.)

The advent of the Christian God, as the maximum god attained so far, was therefore accompanied by the maximum feeling of guilty indebtedness on earth. Presuming we have gradually entered upon the *reverse* course, there is no small probability that with the irresistible decline of faith in the Christian God there is now also a considerable decline in mankind's feeling of guilt; indeed, the prospect cannot be dismissed that the complete and definitive victory of atheism might free mankind of this whole feeling of guilty indebtedness toward its origin, its *causa prima*.[5] Atheism and a kind of *second innocence* belong together.—

---

5. [First cause. —TRANS.]

So much for a first brief preliminary on the connection of the concepts "guilt" and "duty" with religious presuppositions: I have up to now deliberately ignored the moralization of these concepts (their pushing back into the conscience; more precisely, the involvement of the *bad* conscience with the concept of god); and at the end of the last section I even spoke as if this moralization had not taken place at all, and as if these concepts were now necessarily doomed since their presupposition, the faith in our "creditor," in God, had disappeared. The reality is, to a fearful degree, otherwise.

The moralization of the concepts guilt and duty, their being pushed back into the *bad* conscience, actually involves an attempt to *reverse* the direction of the development described above, or at least to bring it to a halt: the *aim* now is to preclude pessimistically, once and for all, the prospect of a final discharge; the *aim* now is to make the glance recoil disconsolately from an iron impossibility; the *aim* now is to turn back the concepts "guilt" and "duty"—back against whom? There can be no doubt: against the "debtor" first of all, in whom from now on the bad conscience is firmly rooted, eating into him and spreading within him like a polyp, until at last the irredeemable debt gives rise to the conception of irredeemable penance, the idea that it cannot be discharged ("*eternal* punishment"). Finally, however, they are turned back against the "creditor," too: whether we think of the *causa prima* of man, the beginning of the human race, its primal ancestor who is from now on burdened with a curse ("Adam," "original sin," "unfreedom of the will"), or of nature from whose womb mankind arose and into whom the principle of evil is projected from now on ("the diabolizing of nature"), or of existence in general, which is now considered *worthless as such* (nihilistic withdrawal from it, a desire for nothingness or a desire for its antithesis, for a different mode of being, Buddhism and the like)—suddenly we stand before the paradoxical and horrifying expedient that afforded temporary relief for tormented humanity, that stroke of genius on the part of Christianity: God himself sacrifices himself for the guilt of mankind, God himself makes payment to himself, God as the only being who can redeem man from what has become unredeemable for man himself—the creditor sacrifices himself for his debtor, out of *love* (can one credit that?), out of love for his debtor!—

You will have guessed *what* has really happened here, *beneath* all this: that will to self-tormenting, that repressed cruelty of the animal-man made inward and scared back into himself, the creature imprisoned in the "state" so as to be tamed, who invented the bad conscience in order to hurt himself after the *more natural* vent for this desire to hurt had been blocked—this man of the bad conscience has seized upon the presupposition of religion so as to drive his self-torture to its most gruesome pitch of severity and rigor. Guilt before *God:* this thought becomes an instrument of torture to him. He apprehends in "God" the ultimate antithesis of his own ineluctable animal instincts; he reinterprets these animal instincts themselves as a form of guilt before God (as hostility, rebellion, insurrection against the "Lord," the "father," the primal ancestor and origin of the world); he stretches himself upon the contradiction "God" and "Devil"; he ejects from himself all his denial of himself, of his nature, naturalness, and actuality, in the form of an affirmation, as something existent, corporeal, real, as God, as the holiness of God, as God the Judge, as God the Hangman, as the beyond, as eternity, as torment without end, as hell, as the immeasurability of punishment and guilt.

In this psychical cruelty there resides a madness of the will which is absolutely unexampled: the *will* of man to find himself guilty and reprehensible to a degree that can never be atoned for; his *will* to think himself punished without any possibility of the punishment becoming equal to the guilt; his *will* to infect and poison the fundamental ground of things with the problem of punishment and guilt so as to cut off once and for all his own exit from this labyrinth of "fixed ideas"; his *will* to erect an ideal—that of the "holy God"—and in the face of it to feel the palpable certainty of his own absolute unworthiness. Oh this insane, pathetic beast—man! What ideas he has, what unnaturalness, what paroxysms of nonsense, what *bestiality of thought* erupts as soon as he is prevented just a little from being a *beast in deed!*

All this is interesting, to excess, but also of a gloomy, black, unnerving sadness, so that one must forcibly forbid oneself to gaze too long into these abysses. Here is *sickness,* beyond any doubt, the most terrible sickness that has ever raged in man; and whoever can still bear to hear (but today one no longer has ears for this!) how in this night of torment and absurdity there has resounded the cry of *love,* the cry of the most nostalgic rapture, of redemption through *love,* will turn away, seized by invincible horror.—There is so much in man that is hideous!—Too long, the earth has been a madhouse!— *sick!*

∞

I regard Christianity as the most fatal seductive lie that has yet existed, as the great unholy lie: I draw out the after-growth and sprouting of its ideal from beneath every form of disguise, I reject every compromise position with respect to it—I force a war against it.

Petty people's morality as the measure of things: this is the most disgusting degeneration culture has yet exhibited. And this kind of ideal still hanging over mankind as "God"!!

The *law,* the thoroughly realistic formalization of certain conditions for the self-preservation of a community, forbids certain actions directed to certain ends, namely those that are directed against the community: it does *not* forbid the disposition that produces these actions—for it needs these actions for other ends, namely against the enemies of the community. Then the moral idealist appears and says: "God beholds the heart: the action itself is nothing; one must exterminate the aggressive disposition that produces it—" Under normal conditions one laughs at this; only in those exceptional instances when a community lives absolutely outside the necessity of waging war for its existence does one lend an ear to such things. One abandons a disposition whose *utility* is no longer apparent.

This was the case, e.g., when Buddha appeared amidst a very peaceable and even spiritually exhausted community.

This was also the case with the earliest Christian community (also Jewish community), whose presupposition is the absolutely unpolitical Jewish society. Christianity could grow only in the soil of Judaism, i.e., amidst a people that had already renounced politics and lived a kind of parasitic existence within the Roman order of things. Christianity is a step further on: one is even more free to "emasculate" oneself—circumstances permit it.

One drives nature out of morality when one says, "Love your enemies": for then the natural "Thou shalt love thy neighbor and hate thy enemy" in the law (in instinct) has become meaningless; then this love of one's neighbor must also find a new basis (as a kind of love of God). Everywhere, God is inserted and utility withdrawn; everywhere the real origin of morality is denied: the veneration of nature, which lies precisely in the recognition of a natural morality, is destroyed at its roots—

The preponderance of an altruistic mode of valuation is the consequence of an instinct that one is ill constituted. The value judgment here is at bottom "I am not worth much": a merely physiological value judgment; even more clearly: the feeling of impotence, the absence of the great affirmative feelings of power (in muscles, nerves, ganglia). This value judgment is translated into a moral or a religious judgment, according to the culture of this class (the predominance of religious and moral judgments is always a sign of a lower culture): it seeks to establish itself by relating to spheres in which it recognizes the concept "value" in general. The interpretation by means of which the Christian sinner believes he understands himself is an attempt to justify his lack of power and self-confidence: he would rather consider himself guilty than feel bad for no reason: it is a symptom of decay to require interpretations of this sort at all.

In other cases, the underprivileged man seeks the reason not in his "guilt" (as the Christian does), but in society: the socialist, the anarchist, the nihilist—in as much as they find their existence something of which someone must be *guilty*, they are still the closest relations of the Christian, who also believes he can better endure his sense of sickness and ill-constitutedness by finding someone whom he can make responsible for it. The instinct of revenge and *ressentiment* appears here in both cases as a means of enduring, as the instinct of self-preservation: just as is the preference for altruistic theory and practice.

Hatred of egoism, whether it be one's own (as with Christians) or another's (as with socialists), is thus revealed as a value judgment under the predominating influence of revenge; on the other hand, as an act of prudence for the self-preservation of the suffering by an enhancement of their feelings of cooperation and solidarity—

Finally, even that release of *ressentiment* in the judging, rejecting, punishing of egoism (one's own or another's) is also, as already indicated, an instinct of self-preservation on the part of the underprivileged. *In summa*: the cult of altruism is a specific form of egoism that regularly appears under certain physiological conditions.

When the socialist with a fine indignation demands "justice," "right," "equal rights," he is merely acting under the impress of his inadequate culture that cannot explain why he is suffering: on the other hand, he enjoys himself; if he felt better he would refrain from crying out: he would then find pleasure in other things. The same applies to the Christian: he condemns, disparages, curses the "world"—himself not excluded. But that is no reason for taking his clamor seriously. In both cases we are in the presence of invalids who feel better for crying out, for whom defamation is a relief.

To ordinary human beings, finally—the vast majority who exist
for service and the general advantage, and who *may* exist only
for that—religion gives an inestimable contentment with their
situation and type, manifold peace of the heart, an ennobling of
obedience, one further happiness and sorrow with their peers
and something transfiguring and beautifying, something of a
justification for the whole everyday character, the whole lowli-
ness, the whole half-brutish poverty of their souls. Religion and
religious significance spread the splendor of the sun over such
ever-toiling human beings and make their own sight tolerable to
them. Religion has the same effect which an Epicurean philosophy has on sufferers of a higher rank: it is refreshing, refining,
makes, as it were, the most of suffering, and in the end even
sanctifies and justifies. Perhaps nothing in Christianity or
Buddhism is as venerable as their art of teaching even the lowli-
est how to place themselves through piety in an illusory higher
order of things and thus to maintain their contentment with the
real order, in which their life is hard enough—and precisely this
hardness is necessary.

In the end, to be sure—to present the other side of the account
of these religions, too, and to expose their uncanny dangerousness—one always pays dearly and terribly when religions do *not*
want to be a means of education and cultivation in the philosopher's hand but insist on having their own *sovereign* way, when
they themselves want to be ultimate ends and not means among
other means. There is among men as in every other animal
species an excess of failures, of the sick, degenerating, infirm,
who suffer necessarily; the successful cases are, among men too,
always the exception—and in view of the fact that man is the *as
yet undetermined animal,* the rare exception. But still worse: the
higher the type of man that a man represents, the greater the
improbability that he will turn out *well*. The accidental, the law
of absurdity in the whole economy of mankind, manifests itself

most horribly in its destructive effect on the higher men whose complicated conditions of life can only be calculated with great subtlety and difficulty.

What, then, is the attitude of the above-mentioned two greatest religions toward this *excess* of cases that did not turn out right? They seek to preserve, to preserve alive whatever can possibly be preserved; indeed, as a matter of principle, they side with these cases as religions for *sufferers;* they agree with all those who suffer life like a sickness and would like to make sure that every other feeling about life should be considered false and should become impossible. Even if the very highest credit is given to this considerate and preserving care, which, besides being directed toward all the others, was and is also directed toward the highest type of man, the type that so far has almost always suffered most; nevertheless, in a total accounting, the *sovereign* religions we have had so far are among the chief causes that have kept the type "man" on a lower rung—they have preserved too much of *what ought to perish.* What we have to thank them for is inestimable; and who could be rich enough in gratitude not to be impoverished in view of all that the "spiritual men" of Christianity, for example, have so far done for Europe! And yet, when they gave comfort to sufferers, courage to the oppressed and despairing, a staff and support to the dependent, and lured away from society into monasteries and penitentiaries for the soul those who had been destroyed inwardly and who had become savage: how much more did they have to do besides, in order to work with a good conscience and on principle, to preserve all that was sick and that suffered—which means, in fact and in truth, to *worsen the European race?* Stand all valuations *on their head—that* is what they had to do. And break the strong, sickly o'er great hopes, cast suspicion on the joy in beauty, bend everything haughty, manly, conquering, domineering, all the instincts characteristic of the highest and best-turned-out type of "man," into unsureness, agony of conscience, self-destruction—indeed, invert all love of the earthly and of dominion over the earth into hatred of the earth and the earthly—*that* is the task the church posed for itself and had to pose, until in its estimation "becoming unworldly," "unsensual," and "higher men" were fused into a single feeling. . . .

I meant to say: Christianity has been the most calamitous kind of arrogance yet. Men, not high and hard enough to have any right to try to form *man* as artists; men, not strong and far-sighted enough to *let* the foreground law of thousandfold failure and ruin prevail, though it cost them sublime self-conquest; men, not noble enough to see the abysmally different order of rank, chasm of rank, between man and man—*such* men have so far held sway over the fate of Europe, with their "equal before God," until finally a smaller, almost ridiculous type, a herd animal, something eager to please, sickly, and mediocre has been bred, the European of today—

∽

Why everything resolved itself into play-acting.—The rudimentary psychology that considered only the *conscious* motives of men (as causes), that took "consciousness" for an attribute of the soul, that sought a will (i.e., an intention) behind all action: it needed, first, only to answer "Happiness" to the question: What do men want? (one dared not say "Power": that would have been immoral);—consequently there is in all the actions of men the intention of attaining happiness. Secondly: if man does in fact not achieve happiness, why is it? Because he blunders in respect of the means.—What is unfailingly the means to happiness? Answer: virtue.—Why virtue?—Because it is supremely rational and because rationality makes it impossible to err in the choice of means: it is as *reason* that virtue is the way to happiness. Dialectic is the constant occupation of virtue, because it excludes all clouding of the intellect and all affects.

In fact, man does *not* want "happiness." Pleasure is a feeling of power: if one excludes the affects, then one excludes the states that give the highest feeling of power, consequently of pleasure. The highest rationality is a cold, clear state very far from giving that feeling of happiness that intoxication of any kind brings with it—

The philosophers of antiquity combat everything that intoxicates—that impairs the absolute coldness and neutrality of the consciousness— They were consistent with their false presupposition: that consciousness is the exalted, the supreme state, the precondition of perfection—whereas the opposite is true——

To the extent that it is willed, to the extent that it is conscious, there is no perfection in action of any kind. The philosophers of antiquity were the greatest duffers in practice because they condemned themselves to be duffers in theory— *In praxi,* everything resolved itself into play-acting;—and whoever saw through this, e.g., Pyrrho, judged as everyone did, namely that in goodness and integrity "little people" were far superior to philosophers.

All the more profound natures of antiquity were disgusted with the philosophers of virtue: they were looked upon as quarrelsome and play actors. (Judgment on Plato: that of Epicurus, that of Pyrrho.)

Result: little people are superior to them in their way of living, in patience, in goodness and mutual assistance:—approximately the claim made by Dostoevsky or Tolstoy for his muzhiks: they are more philosophical in practice, they meet the exigencies of life more courageously—

If one wants a proof of how profoundly and thoroughly the actually barbarous needs of man seek satisfaction, even when he is tamed and "civilized," one should take a look at the "leitmotifs" of the entire evolution of philosophy:—a sort of revenge on reality, a malicious destruction of the valuations by which men live, an unsatisfied soul that feels the tamed state as a torture and finds a voluptuous pleasure in a morbid unraveling of all the bonds that tie it to such a state.

The history of philosophy is a secret raging against the preconditions of life, against the value feelings of life, against partisanship in favor of life. Philosophers have never hesitated to affirm a world provided it contradicted this world and furnished them with a pretext for speaking ill of this world. It has been hitherto the grand school of slander; and it has imposed itself to such an extent that today our science, which proclaims itself the advocate of life, has accepted the basic slanderous position and treated this world as apparent, this chain of causes as merely phenomenal. What is it really that hates here?

I fear it is still the Circe of philosophers, morality, that has here bewitched them into having to be slanderers forever— They believed in moral "truths," they found there the supreme values—what else could they do but deny existence more firmly the more they got to know it?—For this existence is immoral— And this life depends upon immoral preconditions: and all morality *denies* life—.

∽

In late ages that may be proud of their humanity, so much fear remains, so much *superstitious* fear of the "savage cruel beast" whose conquest is the very pride of these more humane ages, that even palpable truths remain unspoken for centuries, as if by some agreement, because they look as if they might reanimate that savage beast one has finally "mortified." Perhaps I dare something when I let one of these truths slip out: let others catch it again and give it "milk of the pious ways of thinking" to drink until it lies still and forgotten in its old corner.

We should reconsider cruelty and open our eyes. We should at long last learn impatience lest such immodest fat errors keep on strutting about virtuously and saucily, as have been fostered about tragedy, for example, by philosophers both ancient and modern. Almost everything we call "higher culture" is based on the spiritualization of *cruelty*, on its becoming more profound: this is my proposition. That "savage animal" has not really been "mortified"; it lives and flourishes, it has merely become—divine.

What constitutes the painful voluptuousness of tragedy is cruelty; what seems agreeable in so-called tragic pity, and at bottom in everything sublime, up to the highest and most delicate shudders of metaphysics, receives its sweetness solely from the admixture of cruelty. What the Roman in the arena, the Christian in the ecstasies of the cross, the Spaniard at an auto-da-fé or bullfight, the Japanese of today when he flocks to tragedies, the laborer in a Parisian suburb who feels a nostalgia for bloody revolutions, the Wagnerienne who "submits to" *Tristan and Isolde,* her will suspended—what all of them enjoy and seek to drink in with mysterious ardor are the spicy potions of the great Circe, "cruelty."

To see this we must, of course, chase away the clumsy psychology of bygone times which had nothing to teach about cruelty except that it came into being at the sight of the sufferings of *others*. There is also an abundant, over-abundant enjoyment at one's own suffering, at making oneself suffer—and wherever man allows himself to be persuaded to self-denial in the *religious* sense, or to self-mutilation, as among Phoenicians and ascetics, or altogether to desensualization, decarnalization, contrition, Puritanical spasms of penitence, vivisection of the conscience, and *sacrifizio dell'intelletto*[6] à la Pascal, he is secretly lured and pushed forward by his cruelty, by those dangerous thrills of cruelty turned *against oneself.*

Finally consider that even the seeker after knowledge forces his spirit to recognize things against the inclination of the spirit, and often enough also against the wishes of his heart—by way of saying No where he would like to say Yes, love, and adore— and thus acts as an artist and transfigurer of cruelty. Indeed, any insistence on profundity and thoroughness is a violation, a desire to hurt the basic will of the spirit which unceasingly strives for the apparent and superficial—in all desire to know there is a drop of cruelty.

---

6. [Sacrifice of the intellect. —TRANS.]

Here belongs also, finally, that by no means unproblematic readiness of the spirit to deceive other spirits and to dissimulate in front of them, that continual urge and surge of a creative, form-giving changeable force: in this the spirit enjoys the multiplicity and craftiness of its masks, it also enjoys the feeling of its security behind them: after all, it is surely its protean arts that defend and conceal it best.

This will to mere appearance, to simplification, to masks, to cloaks, in short, to the surface—for every surface is a cloak—is *countered* by that sublime inclination of the seeker after knowledge who insists on profundity, multiplicity, and thoroughness, with a *will* which is a kind of cruelty of the intellectual conscience and taste. Every courageous thinker will recognize this in himself, assuming only that, as fit, he has hardened and sharpened his eye for himself long enough and that he is used to severe discipline, as well as severe words. He will say, "There is something cruel in the inclination of my spirit"; let the virtuous and kindly try to talk him out of that!

Indeed, it would sound nicer if we were said, whispered, reputed to be distinguished not by cruelty but by "extravagant honesty," we free, *very* free spirits—and perhaps *that* will actually be our posthumous reputation. Meanwhile—for there is plenty of time until then—we ourselves are probably least inclined to put on the garish finery of such moral word tinsels: our whole work so far makes us sick of this taste and its cheerful luxury. These are beautiful, glittering, jingling, festive words: honesty, love of truth, love of wisdom, sacrifice for knowledge, heroism of the truthful—they have something that swells one's pride. But we hermits and marmots have long persuaded ourselves in the full secrecy of a hermit's conscience that this worthy verbal pomp, too, belongs to the old mendacious pomp, junk, and gold dust of unconscious human vanity, and that under such flattering colors and make-up as well, the basic text of *homo natura* must again be recognized.

To translate man back into nature; to become master over the many vain and overly enthusiastic interpretations and connotations that have so far been scrawled and painted over that eternal basic text of *homo natura;* to see to it that man henceforth stands before man as even today, hardened in the discipline of science, he stands before the *rest* of nature, with intrepid Oedipus eyes and sealed Odysseus ears, deaf to the siren songs of old metaphysical bird catchers who have been piping at him all too long, "You are more, you are higher, you are of a different origin!"—that may be a strange and insane task, but it is a *task*—who would deny that? Why did we choose this insane task? Or, putting it differently: "why have knowledge at all?"

Everybody will ask us that. And we, pressed this way, we who have put the same question to ourselves a hundred times, we have found and find no better answer—

A new species of philosophers is coming up: I venture to baptize them with a name that is not free of danger. As I unriddle them, insofar as they allow themselves to be unriddled—for it belongs to their nature to *want* to remain riddles at some point—these philosophers of the future may have a right—it might also be a wrong—to be called *attempters*. This name itself is in the end a mere attempt and, if you will, a temptation.

Are these coming philosophers new friends of "truth"? That is probable enough, for all philosophers so far have loved their truths. But they will certainly not be dogmatists. It must offend their pride, also their taste, if their truth is supposed to be a truth for everyman—which has so far been the secret wish and hidden meaning of all dogmatic aspirations. "My judgment is *my* judgment": no one else is easily entitled to it—that is what such a philosopher of the future may perhaps say of himself.

One must shed the bad taste of wanting to agree with many. "Good" is no longer good when one's neighbor mouths it. And how should there be a "common good"! The term contradicts itself: whatever can be common always has little value. In the

why?

end it must be as it is and always has been: great things remain
for the great, abysses for the profound, nuances and shudders
for the refined, and, in brief, all that is rare for the rare.—

Need I still say expressly after all this that they, too, will be free,
very free spirits, these philosophers of the future—though just
as certainly they will not be merely free spirits but something
more, higher, greater, and thoroughly different that does not
want to be misunderstood and mistaken for something else. But
saying this I feel an *obligation*—almost as much to them as to
ourselves who are their heralds and precursors, we free spirits—
to sweep away a stupid old prejudice and misunderstanding
about the lot of us: all too long it has clouded the concept "free
spirit" like a fog.

In all the countries of Europe, and in America, too, there now
is something that abuses this name: a very narrow, imprisoned,
chained type of spirits who want just about the opposite of
what accords with our intentions and instincts—not to speak of
the fact that regarding the *new* philosophers who are coming up
they must assuredly be closed windows and bolted doors. They
belong, briefly and sadly, among the *levelers*—these falsely so-
called "free spirits"—being eloquent and prolifically scribbling
slaves of the democratic taste and its "modern ideas"; they are
all human beings without solitude, without their own solitude,
clumsy good fellows whom one should not deny either courage
or respectable decency—only they are unfree and ridiculously
superficial, above all in their basic inclination to find in the
forms of the old society as it has existed so far just about the
cause of *all* human misery and failure—which is a way of standing truth happily upon her head! What they would like to strive
for with all their powers is the universal green-pasture happiness of the herd, with security, lack of danger, comfort, and an
easier life for everyone; the two songs and doctrines which they
repeat most often are "equality of rights" and "sympathy for all
that suffers"—and suffering itself they take for something that
must be *abolished*.

We opposite men, having opened our eyes and conscience to the question where and how the plant "man" has so far grown most vigorously to a height—we think that this has happened every time under the opposite conditions, that to this end the dangerousness of his situation must first grow to the point of enormity, his power of invention and simulation (his "spirit") had to develop under prolonged pressure and constraint into refinement and audacity, his life-will had to be enhanced into an unconditional power-will. We think that hardness, forcefulness, slavery, danger in the alley and the heart, life in hiding, stoicism, the art of experiment and devilry of every kind, that everything evil, terrible, tyrannical in man, everything in him that is kin to beasts of prey and serpents, serves the enhancement of the species "man" as much as its opposite does. Indeed, we do not even say enough when we say only that much; and at any rate we are at this point, in what we say and keep silent about, at the *other* end from all modern ideology and herd desiderata—as their antipodes perhaps?

Is it any wonder that we "free spirits" are not exactly the most communicative spirits? that we do not want to betray in every particular *from what* a spirit can liberate himself and *to what* he may then be driven? And as for the meaning of the dangerous formula "beyond good and evil" with which we at least guard against being mistaken for others: we *are* something different from *"libres-penseurs," "liberi pensatori," "Freidenker,"*[7] and whatever else all these goodly advocates of "modern ideas" like to call themselves.

At home, or at least having been guests, in many countries of the spirit; having escaped again and again from the musty agreeable nooks into which preference and prejudice, youth, origin, the accidents of people and books or even exhaustion from wandering seemed to have banished us; full of malice against the lures of dependence that lie hidden in honors, or money, or offices, or enthusiasms of the senses; grateful even to need and

---

7. [Free-thinkers. —TRANS.]

vacillating sickness because they always rid us from some rule and its "prejudice," grateful to god, devil, sheep, and worm in us; curious to a vice, investigators to the point of cruelty, with uninhibited fingers for the unfathomable, with teeth and stomachs for the most indigestible, ready for every feat that requires a sense of acuteness and acute senses, ready for every venture, thanks to an excess of "free will," with fore- and back-souls into whose ultimate intentions nobody can look so easily, with fore- and backgrounds which no foot is likely to explore to the end; concealed under cloaks of light, conquerors even if we look like heirs and prodigals, arrangers and collectors from morning till late, misers of our riches and our crammed drawers, economical in learning and forgetting, inventive in schemas, occasionally proud of tables of categories, occasionally pedants, occasionally night owls of work even in broad daylight; yes, when it is necessary even scarecrows—and today it is necessary; namely, insofar as we are born, sworn, jealous friends of *solitude,* of our own most profound, most midnightly, most mid-daily solitude: that is the type of man we are, we free spirits! And perhaps *you* have something of this, too, you that are coming? you *new* philosophers?—

☞

To revalue values—what would that mean? All the spontaneous—new, future, stronger—movements must be there; but they still appear under false names and valuations and have not yet become conscious of themselves.

A courageous becoming-conscious and affirmation of what has been achieved—a liberation from the slovenly routine of old valuations that dishonor us in the best and strongest things we have achieved.

Every doctrine for which all accumulated energies and explosives are not yet ready at hand, is superfluous. A revaluation of values is achieved only when there is a tension of new needs, of men with new needs, who suffer from the old values without attaining this consciousness.

Points of view for *my* values: whether out of abundance or out of want?—whether one looks on or lends a hand—or looks away and walks off?—whether out of stored-up energy, "spontaneously," or merely stimulated *reactively,* and provoked? whether *simple,* out of a paucity of elements, *or* out of overwhelming mastery over many, so they are pressed into service when they are needed?—whether one is a *problem* or a *solution?*—whether *perfect* with a small task or *imperfect* with an extraordinary goal? whether one is *genuine* or merely an *actor,* whether one is genuine as an actor or merely a copy of an actor, whether one is a "representative" or that which is represented? whether a "personality" or merely a rendezvous of personalities—whether *sick* from sickness or excessive health? whether one goes on ahead as a shepherd or as an "exception" (third species: as a fugitive)? whether one needs *dignity,* or to be a "buffoon"? whether one seeks resistance or avoids it? whether one is imperfect through being "too early" or "too late"? whether by nature one says Yes or No or is a peacock's tail of many colors? whether one is sufficiently proud not to be ashamed even of one's vanity? whether one is still capable of a bite of conscience (this species is becoming rare: formerly the conscience had too much to chew: now it seems to have lost its teeth)? whether one is still capable of a "duty" (there are those who would lose their whole joy in living if their duty were taken from them—especially the womanly, the born subjects)?

It is only a question of strength: to have all the morbid traits of the century, but to balance them through a superabundant, recuperative strength. The strong man. ~

Interpretive Questions
for Discussion

Why does Nietzsche champion the morality of the noble caste—
"barbarians in every terrible sense of the word"—and deride the
slave morality that predominates in the cultures of Europe and
America?

1. Why does Nietzsche want us to think of master behavior as a
   form of morality rather than as immorality or the absence of
   morality? (25–26)

2. Why does Nietzsche maintain that "every enhancement of
   the type 'man' has so far been the work of an aristocratic
   society"? (28) Why does "everything evil, terrible, tyrannical
   in man" serve the enhancement of the species "man" as
   much as its opposite does? (64)

3. Why does Nietzsche say that, although the noble caste in the
   beginning was always the barbarian caste, "their predominance
   did not lie mainly in physical strength but in strength of the
   soul"? (29)

4. Why is the noble man's reverence for his enemies "a bridge to
   love"? Why, according to Nietzsche, is the noble man more capable
   of loving his enemies than the man of *ressentiment* is? (32)

5. Why does Nietzsche compare the nobility, when outside their
   own society, to "uncaged beasts of prey"? Why does he excuse
   their "disgusting" acts of violence and insist that they have an
   "innocent conscience"? (33)

6. Why does Nietzsche say that "together with the fear of man we have also lost our love of him, our reverence for him"? (35)

7. Why does Nietzsche say that "in the days when mankind was not yet ashamed of its cruelty, life on earth was more cheerful than it is now that pessimists exist"? Why does he proclaim that the infliction of suffering is "a genuine seduction *to* life"? (40)

8. Why does Nietzsche insist that the pleasure that comes with power is preferable to the happiness that comes with virtue and the exercise of reason? Why does he suggest that intoxication is preferable to consciousness? (57–58)

Suggested textual analyses
Pages 25–26: beginning, "The noble type of man," and ending, "while the 'bad' are felt to be contemptible."

Pages 28–30: beginning, "Every enhancement of the type 'man,' " and ending, "which is after all the will of life."

According to Nietzsche, why will anyone who understands man's "madness of the will" turn away in horror from the cry of redemption through love?

1. Why do peacefulness and kindness represent "a will to the *denial* of life" when they become the fundamental principle of society? (29)

2. Why does *ressentiment,* in leading the weak to compensate themselves with "an imaginary revenge," become creative and give birth to values? Why, according to Nietzsche, is "the slave revolt in morality" successful? (30)

3. Why does Nietzsche describe man, the inventor of the "bad conscience," as an "animal that rubbed itself raw against the bars of its cage as one tried to 'tame' it"? (43–44)

4. Why has bad conscience "also brought to light an abundance of strange new beauty and affirmation, and perhaps beauty itself"? (46)

5. Why does the moralization of the concepts "guilt" and "duty" lead ultimately to the devaluation of nature and of existence in general? (50–51)

6. Why does Nietzsche regard Christianity "as the most fatal seductive lie that has yet existed, as the great unholy lie"? (52)

7. Why does altruism have its origin in the value judgment "I am not worth much"? Why does the hatred of egoism derive from the desire for revenge and self-preservation? (53–54)

8. Why is what we call "higher culture" based on "the spiritualization of *cruelty,* on its becoming more profound"? (59)

Suggested textual analyses
Pages 46–47: beginning, "One should guard against," and ending, "for the *value* of the unegoistic."

Pages 51–52: beginning, "You will have guessed," and ending, "the earth has been a madhouse!"

What does Nietzsche see as the role of the "free spirits" and "new philosophers," including himself, in creating the future of "man"?

1. Why does Nietzsche think it important to ask what value the value judgments "good" and "evil" themselves have? (24)

2. Is Nietzsche hopeful that a mediation between master morality and slave morality—whether in a single culture or a single soul—can succeed, or must it be based on "the mutual misunderstanding of both"? (25)

3. Why does Nietzsche think that the quest for knowledge and even consciousness itself results from slave morality? (43–44)

4. Why does Nietzsche tell us that the "bad conscience," while not developing *in* the blond beasts of prey, "would not have developed *without them*"? Why does he tell us that "this ugly growth . . . would be lacking if a tremendous quantity of freedom had not been expelled from the world"? (45–46)

5. Why does Nietzsche call man the *"as yet undetermined animal"*? (55)

6. Why, according to Nietzsche, has the history of philosophy heretofore been "the grand school of slander" and a "secret raging" against life? (58–59)

7. Why are the "free spirits" with whom Nietzsche allies himself "born, sworn, jealous friends of *solitude*"? (64–65)

8. Why does Nietzsche say, "It is only a question of strength: to have all the morbid traits of the century, but to balance them through a superabundant, recuperative strength"? (66)

9. Is Nietzsche urging the return to a morality that has been lost in our modern age, or is he taking an amoral stance?

Suggested textual analyses
Pages 63–65: beginning, "In all the countries of Europe," and ending, "you *new* philosophers?—"
Page 66: from "Points of view for *my* values:" to the end of the selection.

FOR FURTHER REFLECTION

1. Is there one morality for everyone, or is morality relative to one's power or lack of power?

2. Does slave morality or master morality have the upper hand in America today? Do you find master morality and slave morality to be confused in your own soul?

3. Can there be friendship between people of unequal power?

4. Are we today, with our emphasis on "equality of rights" and "sympathy for all that suffers," merely seeking the "green-pasture happiness of the herd"? Is it an inherent flaw in democracy that it favors the herd?

5. Are philosophy and religion world-denying expressions of soul-sickness?

6. Is it healthy to live without regrets?

7. Would Nietzsche have looked upon the Nazis as making a valid attempt to enhance the type "man," or would he have condemned their actions as lacking nobility of character?

MOOSBRUGGER

Robert Musil

ROBERT MUSIL (1880–1942), born in
Klagenfurt, Austria, was the only son of
noble parents. Educated for a military career,
Musil changed his mind shortly before being
commissioned (but later served as an officer
in World War I) and began to study civil
engineering, taking his diploma in 1901.
In 1908, he earned a degree in philosophy,
writing his thesis on epistemology. On the
strength of his successful first book, *Young
Törless,* Musil declined several opportunities
to become an academic philosopher in order
to pursue a career as an independent writer.
Nonetheless, he struggled for many years to
both make a living and find the time and
energy for writing. *The Man Without Qualities*
(1930–1943), from which the following
selection is taken, is Musil's magnum opus
and—though unfinished—one of the longest
and most ambitious novels in literature. Ulrich
is the novel's main character. The story of the
sex murderer Moosbrugger fascinates Ulrich
and becomes a recurrent theme of his
reflection upon Austrian society.

THE MOOSBRUGGER CASE was currently much in the news. Moosbrugger was a carpenter, a big man with broad shoulders and no excess fat on him, a head of hair like brown lamb's wool, and good-natured strong paws. His face also expressed a good-natured strength and right-mindedness, qualities one would have smelled (had one not seen them) in the blunt, plain, dry workaday smell that belonged to this thirty-four-year-old man and came from the wood he worked with and a job that called as much for mindfulness as for exertion.

Anyone who came up against this face for the first time, a face blessed by God with every sign of goodness, would stop as if rooted to the spot, because Moosbrugger was usually flanked by two armed guards, his hands shackled with a small, strong steel chain, its grip held by one of his escorts.

When he noticed anyone staring at him a smile would pass over his broad, good-natured face with the unkempt hair and a mustache and the little chin tuft. He wore a short black jacket with light gray trousers, his bearing was military, and he planted his feet wide apart; but it was that smile that most fascinated the reporters in the courtroom. It might be an embarrassed smile or a cunning smile, an ironic, malicious, pained, mad, bloodthirsty, or terrifying smile: they were groping visibly for contradictory expressions and seemed to be searching desperately in that smile for something they obviously could find nowhere else in the man's entire upright appearance.

For Moosbrugger had killed a woman, a prostitute of the lowest type, in a horrifying manner. The reporters described in detail a knife wound in the throat from the larynx to the back of the neck, also the two stab wounds in the breast that penetrated the heart, and the two in the back on the left side, and how both breasts were sliced through so that they could almost be lifted off. The reporters had expressed their revulsion at this, but they did not stop until they had counted thirty-five stabs in the belly and explained the deep slash that reached from the navel to the sacrum, continuing up the back in numerous lesser cuts, while the throat showed marks of strangulation. From such horrors they could not find their way back to Moosbrugger's good-natured face, although they were themselves good-natured men who had nevertheless described what had happened in a factual, expert manner and, evidently, in breathless excitement. They hardly availed themselves of even the most obvious explanation, that the man before them was insane—for Moosbrugger had already been in various mental hospitals several times for similar crimes—even though a good reporter is very well informed on such questions these days; it looked as though they were still reluctant to give up the idea of the villain, to banish the incident from their own world into the world of the insane. Their attitude was matched by that of the psychiatrists, who had already declared him normal just as often as they had declared him not accountable for his actions. There was also the amazing fact that no sooner had they become known than Moosbrugger's pathological excesses were regarded as "finally something interesting for a change" by thousands of people who deplore the sensationalism of the press, from busy officeholders to fourteen-year-old sons to housewives befogged by their domestic cares. While these people of course sighed over such a monstrosity, they were nevertheless more deeply preoccupied with it than with their own life's work. Indeed, it might happen that a punctilious department head or bank manager would say to his sleepy wife at bedtime: "What would you do now if I were a Moosbrugger?"

When Ulrich first laid eyes on that face with its signs of being a child of God above handcuffs, he quickly turned around, slipped a few cigarettes to the sentry at the nearby court building, and asked him about the convoy that had apparently just left the gates; he was told . . . Well, anyway, this is how something of the sort must have happened in earlier times, since it is often reported this way, and Ulrich almost believed it himself; but the contemporary truth was that he had merely read all about it in the newspaper. It was to be a long time before he met Moosbrugger in person, and before that happened he caught sight of him only once during the trial. The probability of experiencing something unusual through the newspapers is much greater than that of experiencing it in person; in other words, the more important things take place today in the abstract, and the more trivial ones in real life.

What Ulrich learned of Moosbrugger's story in this fashion was more or less the following:

Moosbrugger had started out in life as a poor devil, an orphan shepherd boy in a hamlet so small that it did not even have a village street, and his poverty was such that he never dared speak to a girl. Girls were something he could always only look at, even later on when he became an apprentice and then when he was a traveling journeyman. One only need imagine what it must mean when something one craves as naturally as bread or water can only be looked at. After a while one desires it unnaturally. It walks past, skirts swaying around its calves. It climbs over a stile and is visible up to the knees. One looks into its eyes, and they turn opaque. One hears it laugh and turns around quickly, only to look into a face as immovably

79

round as a hole in the ground into which a mouse has just slipped.

So it is understandable that Moosbrugger justified himself even after the first time he killed a girl by saying that he was constantly haunted by spirits calling to him day and night. They threw him out of bed when he slept and bothered him at his work. Then he heard them talking and quarreling with one another day and night. This was no insanity, and Moosbrugger could not bear being called insane, although he himself sometimes dressed up his story a little with bits of remembered sermons, or trimmed it in accordance with the advice on malingering one picks up in prison. But the material to work with was always there, even if it faded a little when his attention wandered.

It had been the same during his years as a journeyman. Work is not easy for a carpenter to find in winter, and Moosbrugger often had no roof over his head for weeks on end. He might have trudged along the road all day to reach a village, only to find no shelter. He would have to keep on marching late into the night. With no money for a meal, he drinks schnapps until two candles light up behind his eyes and the body keeps walking on its own. He would rather not ask for a cot at the shelter, regardless of the hot soup, partly because of the bedbugs and partly because of the offensive red tape; better to pick up a few pennies by begging and crawl into some farmer's haystack for the night. Without asking, of course; what's the point of spending a long time asking when you're only going to be insulted? In the morning, of course, there is often an argument and a charge of assault, vagrancy, and begging, and finally there is an ever-thickening file of such convictions. Each new magistrate opens this file with much pomposity, as if it explained Moosbrugger.

And who considers what it means to go for days and weeks without a proper bath? The skin gets so stiff that it allows only the clumsiest movements, even when one tries to be delicate; under such a crust the living soul itself hardens. The mind may be less affected, it goes on doing the needful after a fashion, burning like a small light in a huge walking lighthouse full of crushed earthworms and grasshoppers, with everything personal squashed inside, and only the fermenting organic matter stalking onward. As he wandered on through the villages, or even on the deserted roads, Moosbrugger would encounter whole processions of women, one now, and another one half an hour later, but even if they appeared at great intervals and had nothing to do with each other, on the whole they were still processions. They were on their way from one village to another, or had just slipped out of the house; they wore thick shawls or jackets that stood out in stiff, snaky lines around their hips; they stepped into warm rooms or drove their children ahead of them, or were on the road so alone that one could have thrown a stone at them like shying at a crow. Moosbrugger asserted that he could not possibly be a sex murderer, because these females had inspired only feelings of aversion in him. This is not implausible—we think we understand a cat, for instance, sitting in front of a cage staring up at a fat, fair canary hopping up and down, or batting a mouse, letting it go, then batting it again, just to see it run away once more; and what is a dog running after a bicycle, biting at it only in play—man's best friend? There is in this attitude toward the living, moving, silently rolling or flitting fellow creature enjoying its own existence something that suggests a deep innate aversion to it. And then what could one do when she started screaming? One could only come to one's senses, or else, if one simply couldn't do that, press her face to the ground and stuff earth into her mouth.

Moosbrugger was only a journeyman carpenter, a man utterly alone, and while he got on well enough with the other men wherever he worked, he never had a friend. Every now and then the most powerful of instincts turned his inner being cruelly outward. But he may have lacked only, as he said, the education and the opportunity to make something different out of this impulse, an angel of mass destruction or a great anarchist, though not the anarchists who band together in secret societies, whom he contemptuously called fakes. He was clearly ill, but even if his obviously pathological nature provided the basis for his attitude, and this isolated him from other men, it somehow seemed to him a stronger and higher sense of his own self. His whole life was a comically and distressingly clumsy struggle to gain by force a recognition of this sense of himself. Even as an apprentice he had once broken the fingers of one master who tried to beat him. He ran away from another with the master's money—in simple justice, as he said. He never stayed anywhere for long. As long as he could keep others at arm's length, as he always did at first, working peacefully, with his big shoulders and few words, he stayed. But as soon as they began to treat him familiarly and without respect, as if they had caught on to him, he packed up and left, seized by an uncanny feeling as though he were not firmly settled inside his skin. Once, he had waited too long. Four bricklayers on a building site had got together to show him who was boss—they would make the scaffolding around the top story give way under him. He could hear them tittering behind his back as they came closer; he hurled himself at them with all his boundless strength, threw one down two flights of stairs, and cut all the tendons in the arms of two others. To be punished for this, he said, had been a shock to his system. He emigrated to Turkey but came back again, because the world was in league against him everywhere; no magic word and no kindness could prevail against this conspiracy.

He had eagerly picked up such phrases in the mental wards and prisons, with scraps of French and Latin stuck in the most unsuitable places as he talked, ever since he had discovered that it was the possession of these languages that gave those in power the right to decide his fate with their "findings." For the same reason, he also did his utmost during hearings to express himself in an exaggerated High German, saying such things as "This must be regarded as the basis for my brutality" or "I had imagined her to be even more vicious than the others of her kind in my usual estimation of them." But when he saw that this failed to make an impression he could rise to the heights of a grand theatrical pose, declaring disdainfully that he was a

"theoretical anarchist" whom the Social Democrats were ready
to rescue at a moment's notice if he chose to accept a favor from
those utterly pernicious Jewish exploiters of the ignorant working class. This would show them that he too had a "discipline,"
a field of his own where the learned presumption of his judges
could not follow him.

Usually this kind of talk brought him high marks for "remarkable intelligence" in the court's judgment, respectful attention to
his words during the proceedings, and tougher sentences; yet
deep down, his flattered vanity regarded these hearings as the
high points of his life. Which is why he hated no one as fervently
as he hated the psychiatrists who imagined they could dismiss
his whole complex personality with a few foreign words, as if
it were for them an everyday affair. As always in such cases,
the medical diagnoses of his mental condition fluctuated under
the pressure of the superior world of juridical concepts, and
Moosbrugger never missed a chance to demonstrate in open
court his own superiority over the psychiatrists, unmasking them
as puffed-up dupes and charlatans who knew nothing at all, and
whom he could trick into placing him in a mental institution
instead of sending him to prison, where he belonged. For he did
not deny what he had done, but simply wanted his deeds understood as the mishaps of an important philosophy of life. It was
those snickering women who were in the forefront of the conspiracy against him. They all had their skirt-chasers and turned
up their noses at a real man's straight talk, if they didn't take it
as a downright insult. He gave them a wide berth as long as he
could, so as not to let them provoke him, but it was not possible
all the time. There are days when a man feels confused and can't
get hold of anything because his hands are sweating with restlessness. If one then has to give in, he can be sure that at the first
step he takes there will be, far up the road like an advance patrol
sent out by the others, one of those poisons on two feet crossing
his path, a cheat who secretly laughs at the man while she saps
his strength and puts on her act for him, if she doesn't do something much worse to him in her unscrupulousness!

And so the end of that night had come, a night of listless boozing, with lots of noise to keep down the inner restlessness. The world can be unsteady even when you aren't drunk. The street walls waver like stage sets behind which something is waiting for its cue. It gets quieter at the edge of town, where you come into the open fields lit by the moon. That was where Moosbrugger had to circle back to get home, and it was there, by the iron bridge, that the girl accosted him. She was one of those girls who hire themselves out to men in the fields, a job-less, runaway housemaid, a little thing of whom all you could see were two gleaming little mouse eyes under her kerchief. Moosbrugger turned her down and quickened his step, but she begged him to take her home with him. Moosbrugger walked: straight ahead, then around a corner, finally helplessly, this way and that; he took big strides, and she ran alongside him; he stopped, she stood there like a shadow. It was as if he were drawing her along behind him. He made one more attempt to drive her off: he suddenly turned around and spat twice in her face. It was no use; she was invulnerable.

This happened in the immense park, which they had to cross at its narrowest part. Moosbrugger began to feel sure that the girl had a protector nearby—how else would she have the nerve to keep after him despite his exasperation? He reached for the knife in his pants pocket; he wasn't anyone's fool! They might jump him together; behind those bitches the other man was always hiding to jeer at you. Come to think of it, didn't she look like a man in disguise? He saw shadows move and heard crack-ling in the bushes, while this schemer beside him repeated her plea again and again, at regular intervals like a gigantic pendu-lum. But he could see nothing to hurl his giant's strength at, and the uncanny way nothing at all was happening began to frighten him.

By the time they turned into the first, still very dark street, there were beads of sweat on his forehead, and he was trem-bling. He kept his eyes straight ahead and walked into the first café that was still open. He gulped down a black coffee and three brandies and could sit there in peace, for fifteen minutes or so; but when he paid his check the worry was there again: what would he do if she was waiting for him outside? There are such thoughts, like string winding in endless snares around arms and legs. He had hardly taken a few steps on the dark street when he felt the girl at his side. Now she was no longer humble but cocky and self-confident; nor did she plead anymore but merely kept silent. Then he realized that he would never get rid of her, because it was he himself who was drawing her after him. His throat filled up with tearful disgust. He kept walking, and that creature, trailing him, was himself again. It was just the same as when he was always meeting those processions of women in the road. Once, he had cut a big wooden splinter out of his own leg because he was too impatient to wait for the doctor; in the same way, he now felt his knife lying long and hard in his pocket.

But by a superhuman exertion of his moral sense, Moosbrugger hit upon one more way out. Behind the board fence along which the road now led was a playing field; one couldn't be seen there, and so he went in. He lay down in the cramped ticket booth and pushed his head into the corner where it was darkest; the soft, accursed second self lay down beside him. So he pretended to fall asleep right away, in order to be able to sneak out later on. But when he started to creep out softly, feet first, there it was again, winding its arms around his neck. Then he felt something hard, in her pocket or his. He tugged it out. He couldn't say whether it was a scissors or a knife; he stabbed her with it. He had claimed it was only a pair of scissors, but it was his own knife. She fell with her head inside the booth. He dragged her partway outside, onto the soft ground, and kept on stabbing her until he had completely separated her from himself. Then he stood there beside her for maybe another quarter of an hour, looking down at her, while the night grew calmer again and wonderfully smooth. Now she could never again insult a man and trail after him. He finally carried the corpse across the street and laid it down in front of a bush so that it could be more easily found and buried, as he stated, because now it was no longer her fault.

During his trial Moosbrugger created the most unpredictable problems for his lawyer. He sat relaxed on his bench, like a spectator, and called out "Bravo!" every time the prosecutor made a point of what a public menace the defendant was, which Moosbrugger regarded as worthy of him, and gave out good marks to witnesses who declared that they had never noticed anything about him to indicate that he could not be held responsible for his actions.

"You're quite a character," the presiding judge flattered him from time to time, humoring him along as he conscientiously tightened the noose the accused had put around his own neck. At such moments Moosbrugger looked astonished, like a harried bull in the arena, let his eyes wander, and noticed in the faces around him, though he could not understand it, that he had again worked himself one level deeper into his guilt.

Ulrich was especially taken with the fact that Moosbrugger's defense was evidently based on some dimly discernible principle. He had not gone out with intent to kill, nor did his dignity permit him to plead insanity. There could be no question of lust as a motive—he had felt only disgust and contempt. The act could accordingly only be called manslaughter, to which he had been induced by the suspicious conduct of "this caricature of a woman," as he put it. If one understood him rightly, he even wanted the killing to be regarded as a political crime, and he sometimes gave the impression that he was fighting not for himself but for this view of the legal issue. The judge's tactics against him were based on the usual assumption that he was dealing with a murderer's obvious, cunning efforts to evade responsibility.

"Why did you wipe the blood off your hands? Why did you throw the knife away? Why did you change into fresh underwear and clean clothes afterward? Because it was Sunday? Not because you were covered with blood? Why did you go out looking for entertainment? So the crime didn't prevent you from doing so? Did you feel any remorse at all?" Ulrich well understood the deep resignation with which Moosbrugger at such moments lamented his lack of an education, which left him helpless to undo the knots in this net woven of incomprehension. The judge translated this into an emphatic reproof: "You always find a way to shift the blame to others!"

This judge added it all up, starting with the police record and the vagrancy, and presented it as Moosbrugger's guilt, while to Moosbrugger it was a series of completely separate incidents having nothing to do with one another, each of which had a different cause that lay outside Moosbrugger somewhere in the world as a whole. In the judge's eyes, Moosbrugger was the source of his acts; in Moosbrugger's eyes they had perched on him like birds that had flown in from somewhere or other. To the judge, Moosbrugger was a special case; for himself he was a universe, and it was very hard to say something convincing about a universe. Two strategies were here locked in combat, two integral positions, two sets of logical consistency. But Moosbrugger had the less favorable position; even a much cleverer man could not have expressed the strange, shadowy reasonings of his mind. They rose directly out of the confused isolation of his life, and while all other lives exist in hundreds of ways—perceived the same way by those who lead them and by all others, who confirm them—his own true life existed only for him. It was a vapor, always losing and changing shape. He might, of course, have asked his judges whether their lives were essentially different. But he thought no such thing. Standing before the court, everything that had happened so naturally in sequence was now senselessly jumbled up inside him, and he made the greatest efforts to make such sense of it as would be no less worthy than the arguments of his distinguished opponents. The judge seemed almost kindly as he lent support to this effort, offering a helpful word or idea, even if these turned out later to have the most terrible consequences for Moosbrugger.

It was like the struggle of a shadow with a wall, and in the end Moosbrugger's shadow was reduced to a lurid flickering.

Ulrich was present on the last day of the trial. When the presiding judge read out the psychiatrists' findings that the accused was responsible for his actions, Moosbrugger rose to his feet and announced to the court: "I am satisfied with this opinion and have achieved my purpose." The response of scornful incredulity in the eyes around him made him add angrily: "Since it is I who forced the indictment, I declare myself satisfied with the conduct of the case." The presiding judge, who had now become all strictness and retribution, reprimanded him with the remark that the court was not concerned with giving him satisfaction. Then he read him the death sentence, exactly as if it were now time to answer seriously the nonsense Moosbrugger had been spouting throughout the trial, to the amusement of the spectators. Moosbrugger said nothing to this, so that he would not appear to be frightened. Then the proceedings were concluded and it was all over. His mind reeled; he fell back, helpless against the arrogance of those who failed to understand. Even as the guards were leading him out, he turned around, struggling for words, raised his hands in the air, and cried out, in a voice that shook him free of his guards' grip: "I am satisfied, even though I must confess to you that you have condemned a madman."

That was a non sequitur, but Ulrich sat there breathless. This was clearly madness, and just as clearly it was no more than a distortion of our own elements of being. Cracked and obscure it was; it somehow occurred to Ulrich that if mankind could dream as a whole, that dream would be Moosbrugger. Ulrich came back to reality only when "that miserable clown of a lawyer," as Moosbrugger ungratefully referred to him during the trial, announced that he would appeal to have the verdict set aside on grounds of some detail or other, while his towering client was led away.

∞

Suddenly Ulrich's thoughts focused, and as though he were looking through a chink between them, he saw Christian Moosbrugger, the carpenter, and his judges.

In a manner that was painfully ridiculous to anyone not of his mind, the judge spoke:

"Why did you wipe the blood off your hands?—Why did you throw the knife away?—Why did you change into a clean suit and underwear and clean clothes afterward?—Because it was Sunday? Not because they were bloodstained?—How could you go to a dance that same evening? What you had done did not prevent you from going out for a good time? Did you feel no remorse whatsoever?"

Something flickers in Moosbrugger's mind—old prison wisdom: Feign remorse. The flicker gives a twist to his mouth and he says: "Of course I did!"

"But at the police station you said: 'I feel no remorse at all, only such hate and rage I could explode!' " the judge caught him out.

"That may be so," Moosbrugger says, recovering himself and his dignity, "it may be that I had no other feelings then."

"You are a big, strong man," the prosecutor cuts in, "how could you possibly have been afraid of a girl like Hedwig?"

"Your Honor," Moosbrugger answers with a smile, "she was making up to me. She threatened to be even more treacherous than I usually expected women of her sort to be. I may look strong, and I am—"

"Well then," the presiding judge growls, leafing through his files.

"But in certain situations," Moosbrugger says loudly, "I am very shy, even cowardly."

The judge's eyes dart up from the file; like two birds taking off from a branch, they abandon the sentence they had just been perching on.

"But the time you picked that fight with the men on the building site you weren't at all cowardly!" the judge says. "You threw one of them down two floors, you pulled a knife on the others—"

"Your Honor," Moosbrugger cries out in a threatening voice, "I still stand today on the standpoint—"

The presiding judge waves this away.

"Injustice," Moosbrugger says, "must be the basis of my brutality. I have stood before the court, a simple man, and thought Your Honor must know everything anyway. But you have let me down!"

The judge's face had long been buried again in the file.

The prosecutor smiles and says in a kindly tone: "But surely Hedwig was a perfectly harmless girl?"

"Not to me she wasn't!" Moosbrugger says, still indignant.

"It seems to *me*," the presiding judge says emphatically, "that you always manage to put the blame on someone else."

"Now tell me, why did you start stabbing her?" the prosecutor gently begins at the beginning again.

☙

Was it something he had heard at the session of the trial he attended, or had he just picked it up from the reports he had read? He remembered it all so vividly now, as though he could actually hear these voices. He had never in his life "heard voices"—by God, he was not like that. But if one does hear them, then something descends like the quiet peace of a snowfall. Suddenly walls are there, from the earth to the sky; where before there was air, one strides through thick soft walls, and all the voices that hopped from one place to another in the cage of the air now move about freely within the white walls that have fused together down to their inmost essence.

He was probably overstimulated from work and boredom; such things happen sometimes; anyway, he didn't find it half bad, hearing voices. Suddenly he was saying under his breath, "We have a second home, where everything we do is innocent."

Bonadea[1] was lacing up a string. She had meanwhile come into his room. She was displeased with their conversation; she found it in poor taste. She had long since forgotten the name of the man who had killed that girl, the case the papers had been so full of, and it all came back to mind only reluctantly when Ulrich began to speak of him.

"But if Moosbrugger can evoke this disturbing impression of innocence," he said after a while, "how much more innocent that poor, ragged, shivering creature was, with those mouse eyes under that kerchief, that Hedwig, who begged him for a night's shelter in his room and got herself killed for it."

"Must you?" Bonadea offered and shrugged her white shoulders. For when Ulrich gave this turn to the conversation, it came at the maliciously chosen moment when the clothes his offended friend had half put on when she came into his room, thirsting for reconciliation, were once more heaped on the carpet, forming a small, charmingly mythological crater of foam like the one that had given birth to Aphrodite. Bonadea was therefore ready to detest Moosbrugger, and to pass over the fate of his victim with a fleeting shudder. But Ulrich would not let it go at that, and insisted on vividly depicting for her Moosbrugger's impending fate.

"Two men who have no bad feelings against him at all will put the noose around his neck, only because that is what they are paid for. Perhaps a hundred people will be watching, some because it is their job, others because everyone wants to have seen an execution once in his life. A solemn gentleman in a top hat, frock coat, and black gloves will then tighten the noose, while at the same moment his helpers grab hold of Moosbrugger's legs and pull, to break his neck. Then the man with the black gloves plays doctor, and lays a hand on Moosbrugger's heart to check whether it is still beating—because if it is, the

---

1. [Ulrich's mistress.]

whole procedure has to be gone through once again, more impatiently and with less solemnity. Now, are you really for Moosbrugger or against him?" Ulrich asked.

Slowly and painfully, like a person awakened at the wrong time, Bonadea had lost "the mood," as she was accustomed to calling her fits of adultery. Now, after her hands had irresolutely held her slipping clothes and open corset for a while, she had to sit down. Like every woman in a similar situation, she had firm confidence in an established public order of such a degree of justice that one could go about one's private affairs without having to think about it. But now, reminded of the opposite, compassionate partisanship for Moosbrugger as victim took hold of her, sweeping aside any thought of Moosbrugger the criminal.

"Then you are always for the victim," Ulrich insisted, "and against the act?"

Bonadea expressed the obvious feeling that such a conversation in such a situation was not appropriate.

"But if your judgment is so consistent in condemning the act," Ulrich replied, instead of instantly apologizing, "then how can you justify your adulteries, Bonadea?"

It was the plural that was in such especially bad taste! Bonadea said nothing but sat down, with a disdainful look, in one of the luxurious armchairs and stared up, insulted, at the dividing line between wall and ceiling.

It is not advisable to feel kinship with an obvious lunatic, nor did Ulrich do so. And yet why did one expert maintain that Moosbrugger was a lunatic and the other that he was not? Where had the reporters got their slickly factual account of the work of Moosbrugger's knife? And by what qualities did Moosbrugger arouse that excitement and horror that made half of the two million people who lived in this city react to him as if he were a family quarrel or a broken engagement, something so personally exciting that it stirred normally dormant areas of the soul, while his story was a more indifferent novelty in the country towns and meant nothing at all in Berlin or Breslau, where from time to time they had their own Moosbruggers, the Moosbruggers in their own families, to think about. The awful way society had of toying with its victims preoccupied Ulrich. He felt an echo of it in himself too. No impulse stirred in him either to free Moosbrugger or to assist justice, and his feelings stood on end like a cat's fur. For some unknown reason Moosbrugger concerned him more deeply than the life he himself was leading. Moosbrugger seized him like an obscure poem in which everything is slightly distorted and displaced, and reveals a drifting meaning fragmented in the depths of the mind.

"Thrill-seeking!" He pulled himself up short. To be fascinated with the gruesome or the taboo, in the admissible form of dreams and neuroses, seemed quite in character for the people of the bourgeois age. "Either/or!" he thought. "Either I like you or I don't. Either I defend you, freakishness and all, or I ought to punch myself in the jaw for playing around with this monstrosity!" And finally, a cool but energetic compassion would also be appropriate here. There was a lot that could be done in this day and age to prevent such events and such characters from happening, if only society would make half the moral effort it demands of such victims. But then it turned out that there was yet another angle from which the matter could be considered, and strange memories rose up in Ulrich's mind.

We never judge an act by that aspect of it which is pleasing or displeasing to God. It was Luther, oddly enough, who had said that, probably under the influence of one of the mystics with whom he was friends for a while. It could certainly have been said by many another religious. They were, in the bourgeois sense, all immoralists. They distinguished between the sins and the soul, which can remain immaculate despite the sins, almost as Machiavelli distinguished the ends from the means. The "human heart" had been "taken from them." "In Christ too there was an outer and an inner man, and everything he did with regard to outward things he did as the outer man, while his inner man stood by in immovable solitude," says Eckhart. Such saints and believers would in the end have been capable of acquitting even Moosbrugger! Mankind has certainly made progress since then, but even though it will kill Moosbrugger, it still has the weakness to venerate those men who might—who knows?—have acquitted him.

And now Ulrich remembered a sentence, which was preceded by a wave of uneasiness: "The soul of the Sodomite might pass through the throng without misgiving, and with a child's limpid smile in its eyes; for everything depends on an invisible principle." This was not so very different from the other sayings, yet in its slight exaggeration it had the sweet, sickly breath of corruption. And as it turned out, a space belonged to this saying, a room with yellow French paperbacks on the tables and glass-bead curtains instead of doors; and a feeling stirred in his chest as when a hand reaches inside the split carcass of a chicken to pull out the heart. . . .

∽

The killer of a prostitute, Christian Moosbrugger, had been forgotten a few days after the newspapers stopped printing the reports of his trial, and the public had turned to other things for excitement. Only a circle of experts still took an interest in him. His lawyer had entered a plea to have the trial invalidated, demanded a new psychiatric examination, and taken other steps as well: the execution was indefinitely postponed and Moosbrugger moved to another prison.

The precautions with which this was done flattered him: loaded guns, many people, arms and legs in irons. They were paying attention to him, they were afraid of him, and Moosbrugger loved it. When he climbed into the prison van, he glanced around for admiration and tried to catch the surprised gaze of the passersby. Cold wind, blowing down the street, played with his curly hair; the air drained him. Two seconds; then a guard shoved his behind into the van.

Moosbrugger was vain. He did not like to be pushed like that; he was afraid that the guards would punch him, shout or laugh at him. The fettered giant did not dare to look at any of his escorts and slid to the front of the van of his own accord.

But he was not afraid of death. Life is full of things that must be endured, and that certainly hurt more than being hanged, and whether a man has a few years more or less to live really doesn't matter. The passive pride of a man who has been locked up for long stretches would not let him fear his punishment; but in any case, he did not cling to life. What was there in life that he should love? Surely not the spring breeze, or the open road, or the sun? They only make a man tired, hot, and dusty. No one loves life who really knows it. "If I could say to someone," Moosbrugger thought, " 'Yesterday I had some terrific roast pork at the corner restaurant!' that might be something." But one could do without even that. What would have pleased him was something that could satisfy his ambition, which had always come up against nothing but stupid insults.

An uneven jolting ran from the wheels through the bench into his body. Behind the bars in the door the cobblestones were running backward; heavy wagons were left behind; at times, men, women, or children stumbled diagonally across the bars; a distant cab was gaining on them, growing, coming closer, beginning to spray out life as an anvil throws off sparks; the horses' heads seemed to be about to push through the door; then the clatter of hooves and the soft sound of rubber-tired wheels ran on past behind the wall of the van. Moosbrugger slowly turned his head back to stare again at the ceiling where it met the van's side in front of him. The noises outside roared, blared, were stretched like a canvas over which now and then flitted the shadow of something happening. Moosbrugger took the ride as a change, without paying much attention to its meaning. Between two dark, inert stretches in prison a quarter of an hour's opaque, white, foaming time was shooting by. This was how he had always experienced his freedom. Not really pretty. "That business about the last meal," he thought, "the prison chaplain, the hangmen, the quarter hour before it's all over, won't be too different. It will bounce along on wheels too; I'll be kept busy all the time, like now, trying to keep from sliding off this bench at every jolt, and I won't be seeing or hearing much of anything with all those people hopping around me. It's the best thing that can happen: finally I'll get some peace."

A man who has liberated himself from wanting to live feels immensely superior. Moosbrugger remembered the superintendent who had been his first interrogator at the police station. A real gent, who spoke in a low voice.

"Look here, Mr. Moosbrugger," he had said, "I beseech you: grant me success!" And Moosbrugger had replied, "Well, if success means that much to you, let's draw up a statement."

The judge, later on, was skeptical, but the superintendent had confirmed it in court. "Even if you don't care about relieving your conscience on your own account, please give me the personal satisfaction that you are doing it for my sake." The superintendent had repeated this before the whole court, even the presiding judge had looked pleased, and Moosbrugger had risen to his feet:

"My deep respect to His Honor the superintendent for making this statement!" he had loudly proclaimed, then added, with a graceful bow: "Although the superintendent's last words to me were 'We will probably never see each other again,' it is an honor and a privilege to see you, the superintendent, again today."

A smile of self-approval transformed Moosbrugger's face, and he forgot the guards sitting opposite him, flung to and fro like himself by the jolting van.

∞

Moosbrugger had settled down in his new prison as best he could. The gate had hardly shut behind him when he was bellowed at. He had been threatened with a beating when he protested, if he remembered rightly. He had been put in solitary.

For his walk in the yard he was handcuffed, and the guards' eyes were glued to him. They had shaved his head, even though his sentence was under appeal and not yet legally in force, because, they said, they had to take his measurements. They had lathered him all over with a stinking soft soap, on the pretext of disinfecting him. As an old hand, he knew that all this was against regulations, but behind that iron gate it is not so easy to maintain one's dignity. They did as they pleased with him. He demanded to see the warden, and complained. The warden had to admit that some things were not in accordance with regulations, but it was not a punishment, he said, only a precaution. Moosbrugger complained to the prison chaplain, but the chaplain was a kindly old man whose amiable ministry was anachronistically flawed by his inability to cope with sexual crimes. He abhorred them with the lack of understanding of a body that had never even touched the periphery of such feelings, and was even dismayed that Moosbrugger's honest appearance moved him to the weakness of feeling personally sorry for him. He sent Moosbrugger to the prison doctor, and for his own part, as in all such cases, sent up to the Creator an omnibus prayer that did not go into detail but dealt in such general terms with man's proneness to error that Moosbrugger was included in the moment of prayer along with the freethinkers and atheists. The prison doctor told Moosbrugger that he was making a mountain out of a molehill, gave him a friendly slap on the back, and absolutely refused to pay any attention to his complaints, on the grounds that—if Moosbrugger understood him right—it was all beside the point as long as the question of whether he was insane or only malingering had not been settled by the medical authorities. Infuriated, Moosbrugger suspected that all these people spoke to suit themselves, and that it was this trick with words that gave them the power to do as they pleased with him. He had the feeling of simple people that the educated ought to have their tongues cut out. He looked at the doctor's face with its dueling scars; at the priest's face, withered from the inside; at the austerely tidy office face of the warden; saw each face looking back at him in its own way, and saw in all of them something beyond his reach that they had in common, which had been his lifelong enemy. The constricting pressure that in the outside world forces every person, with all his self-conceit, to wedge himself with effort among all that other flesh, was somewhat eased—despite all the discipline—under the roof of the prison, where everything lived for waiting, and the interaction of the inmates, even when it was coarse and violent, was undermined by a shadow of unreality. Moosbrugger reacted with his whole powerful body to the slackening of tension after the trial. He felt like a loose tooth. His skin itched. He felt miserable, as if he had caught an infection. It was a self-pitying, tenderly nervous hypersensitivity that came over him sometimes: the woman who lay underground and who had got him into this mess seemed to him a crude, nasty bitch contrasted with a child, if he compared her to himself.

Just the same, Moosbrugger was not altogether dissatisfied. He could tell in many ways that he was a person of some importance here, and it flattered him. Even the attention given to all convicts alike gave him satisfaction. The state had to feed them, bathe them, clothe them, and concern itself with their work, their health, their books, and their songs from the moment they had broken the law; it had never done these things before. Moosbrugger enjoyed this attention, even if it was strict, like a child who has succeeded in forcing its mother to notice it with anger. But he did not want it to continue much longer. The idea that his sentence might be commuted to life in prison or in a lunatic asylum sparked in him the resistance we feel when every effort to escape from our circumstances only leads us back to them, time and again. He knew that his lawyer was trying to get the case reopened, that he was to be interrogated all over again, but he made up his mind to oppose that as soon as he could and insist that they kill him.

Above all, he had to make a dignified exit, for his life had been a battle for his rights. In solitary, Moosbrugger considered what his rights were. He couldn't say. But they were everything he had been cheated of all his life. The moment he thought of that he swelled with emotion. His tongue arched and started to move like a Lippizaner stallion in his zeal to pronounce the word nobly enough. "My right," he thought, drawing the word out as long as he could, to realize this concept, and thought, as if he were speaking to someone: "It's when you haven't done anything wrong, or something like that, isn't it?" Suddenly he had it: "Right is justice." That was it. His right was his justice! He looked at his wood-plank bed in order to sit on it, turned awkwardly around to tug at it—in vain, as it was screwed to the floor—then slowly sat down.

He had been cheated of his justice! He remembered his master's wife, when he was sixteen. He had dreamed that something cold was blowing on his belly, then it had disappeared inside his body; he had yelled and fallen out of bed, and the next morning felt as if he had been beaten black-and-blue. Other apprentices had once told him that you could always get a woman by showing her your fist with the thumb sticking out between the middle and the forefinger. He didn't know what to make of it; they all said they had tried it, but when he thought about it the ground gave way under him, or his head seemed to be screwed on wrong; in short, something was going on inside him that separated him by a hairbreadth from the natural order and was not quite steady. "Missus," he said, "I'd like to do something nice to you. . . ." They were alone; she looked into his eyes and must have seen something there; she said: "You just clear out of this kitchen!" He then held up his fist with the thumb sticking out. But the magic worked only halfway: her face turned dark red and she hit him with the wooden ladle in her hand, too fast for him to dodge the blow, right across the face; he realized it only when the blood began to trickle over his lips. But he remembered that instant vividly now, for the blood suddenly turned and flowed upward, up above his eyes, and he threw himself on the strapping woman who had so viciously insulted him; the master came in; and what happened then, until the moment he stood in the street with his legs buckling and his things thrown after him, was like a big red cloth being ripped to shreds. That was how they made a mockery and a shambles of his right, and he took to the road again. Can a man find his rights on the road? All the women were already somebody else's right, and so were all the apples and all the beds. And the police and the judges were worse than the dogs.

But what it really was that always gave people a hold on him, and why they were always throwing him in jails or madhouses, Moosbrugger could never really figure out. He stared long and hard at the floor, at the corners of his cell; he felt like a man who has dropped a key on the floor. But he couldn't find it; the floor and the corners turned day-gray and ordinary again, though just a while ago they had been a dreamscape where a thing or a person springs up at the drop of a word.

Moosbrugger mustered all his logic. He could only remember distinctly all the places it began. He could have ticked them off on his fingers and described them. Once, it had been in Linz, another time in Brăila. Years had passed between. And the last time it was here in the city. He could see every stone so sharply outlined, as stones usually aren't. He also remembered the rotten feeling that always went with it, as if he had poison instead of blood in his veins, or something like that. For instance, he was working outdoors and women passed by; he didn't want to look at them, because they bothered him, but new ones kept constantly passing by, so finally his eyes would follow them with loathing, and that slow turning of his eyes this way and that felt as if his eyes were stirring in tar or in setting cement inside him. Then he noticed that his thoughts were growing heavy. He thought slowly anyway, the words gave him trouble, he never had enough words, and sometimes, when he was talking to someone, the other man would look at him in surprise: he wouldn't understand how much was being said in the one word Moosbrugger was uttering so slowly. He envied all those people who had learned to talk easily when they were young. His own words seemed to stick to his gums to spite him just when he needed them most, and it sometimes took forever to tear out the next syllable so he could go on from there. There was no getting around it: this couldn't be due to natural causes. But when he said in court that it was the Freemasons or the Jesuits or the Socialists who were torturing him this way, nobody understood what he was talking about. Those lawyers and judges could outtalk him, all right, and had all sorts of things to say against him, but none of them had a clue to what was really going on.

When this sort of thing had continued for some time, Moosbrugger got frightened. Just try standing in the street with your hands tied, waiting to see what people will do! He knew that his tongue, or something deep inside him, was glued down, and it made him miserably unsure of himself, a feeling he had to struggle for days to hide. But then there came a sharp, one could almost say soundless, boundary. Suddenly a cold breeze was there. Or else a big balloon rose up in the air right in front of him and flew into his chest. At the same instant he felt something in his eyes, his lips, the muscles of his face; everything around him seemed to fade, to turn black, and while the houses lay down on the trees, some cats quickly leapt from the bushes and scurried away. This lasted only for an instant, then it was over.

This was the real beginning of the time they all wanted to know about and never stopped talking about. They pestered him with the most pointless questions; unfortunately, he could remember his experiences only dimly, through what they meant to him. Because these periods were all meaning! They sometimes lasted for minutes, sometimes for days on end, and sometimes they changed into other, similar experiences that could last for months. To begin with the latter, because they are simpler, and in Moosbrugger's opinion even a judge could understand them: Moosbrugger heard voices or music or a wind, or a blowing and humming, a whizzing and rattling, or shots, thunder, laughing, shouts, speaking, or whispering. It came at him from every direction; the sounds were in the walls, in the air, in his clothes, in his body. He had the impression he was carrying it in his body as long as it was silent; once it was out, it hid somewhere in his surroundings, but never very far from him. When he was working, the voices would speak at him mostly in random words or short phrases, insulting and nagging him, and when he thought of something they came out with it before he could, or spitefully said the opposite of what he meant. It was ridiculous to be declared insane on this account; Moosbrugger regarded these voices and visions as mere monkeyshines. It entertained him to hear and see what they did; that was ever so much better than the hard, heavy thoughts he had himself. But of course he got very angry when they really annoyed him, that was only natural. Moosbrugger knew, because he always paid close attention to all the expressions that were applied to him, that this was called hallucinating, and he was pleased that he had this knack for hallucination that others lacked; it enabled him to see all sorts of things others didn't, such as lovely landscapes and hellish monsters. But he found that they always made far too much of it, and when the stays in mental hospitals became too unpleasant, he maintained outright that he was only pretending. The know-it-alls would ask him how loud the sounds were; a senseless question, because of course what he heard was sometimes as loud as a thunderclap, and sometimes the merest whisper. Even the physical pains that sometimes plagued him could be unbearable or slight enough to be imaginary. That wasn't the important thing. Often he could not have described exactly what he saw, heard, and felt, but he knew what it was. It could be very blurred; the visions came from outside, but a shimmer of observation told him at the same time that they were really something inside himself. The important thing was that it is not at all important whether something is inside or outside; in his condition, it was like clear water on both sides of a transparent sheet of glass.

When he was feeling on top of things Moosbrugger paid no attention at all to his voices and visions but spent his time in thinking. He called it thinking because he had always been impressed with the word. He thought better than other people because he thought both inside and outside. Thinking went on inside him against his will. He said that thoughts were planted in him. He was hypersensitive to the merest trifles, as a woman is when her breasts are tight with milk, but this did not interfere with his slow, manly reflectiveness. At such times his thoughts flowed like a stream running through a lush meadow swelled by hundreds of leaping brooks.

Now Moosbrugger had let his head drop and was looking down at the wood between his fingers. "A squirrel in these parts is called a tree kitten," it occurred to him, "but just let somebody try to talk about a tree cat with a straight face! Everyone would prick up their ears as if a real shot had gone off among the farting sound of blanks on maneuvers. In Hesse, on the other hand, it's called a tree fox. Any man who's traveled around knows such things."

But oh, how curious the psychiatrists got when they showed him a picture of a squirrel and he said: "That's a fox, I guess, or it could be a hare, or maybe a cat or something." They'd always shoot a question right back at him then: "How much is fourteen plus fourteen?" and he would say in his deliberate way, "Oh, about twenty-eight to forty." This "about" gave them trouble, which made Moosbrugger grin. It was really so simple. He knew perfectly well that you get twenty-eight when you go on from fourteen to another fourteen; but who says you have to stop there? Moosbrugger's gaze would always range a little farther ahead, like that of a man who has reached the top of a ridge outlined against the sky and finds that behind it there are other, similar ridges. And if a tree kitten is no cat and no fox, and has teeth like a hare's, and the fox eats the hare, you don't have to be so particular about what you call it; you just know it's somehow sewn together out of all those things and goes scampering over the trees. Moosbrugger's experience and conviction were that no thing could be singled out by itself, because things hang together. It had happened that he said to a girl, "Your sweet rose lips," but suddenly the words gave way at their seams and something upsetting happened: her face went gray, like earth veiled in a mist, there was a rose sticking out of it on a long stem, and the temptation to take a knife and cut it off, or punch it back into the face, was overwhelming. Of course, Moosbrugger did not always go for his knife; he only did that when he couldn't get rid of the temptation any other way. Usually he used all his enormous strength to hold the world together.

In a good mood, he could look a man in the face and see in it his own face, as it might gaze back at him from among the minnows and bright pebbles of a shallow stream; in a bad mood, he could tell by a fleeting glance at a man's face that here was the same man who always gave him trouble, everywhere, no matter how differently he disguised himself each time. How can anyone object to this? We all have trouble with the same man almost every time. If we were to investigate who the people are we get so idiotically fixated on, it is bound to turn out to be the one with the lock to which we have the key. And in love? How many people look at the same beloved face day in, day out, yet when they shut their eyes can't say what it looks like? Or even aside from love and hate; how incessantly things are subject to change, depending on habit, mood, point of view! How often joy burns out and an indestructible core of sadness emerges! How often a man calmly beats up another, whom he might as easily leave in peace. Life forms a surface that acts as if it could not be otherwise, but under its skin things are pounding and pulsing. Moosbrugger always kept his legs solidly planted on real earth, holding them together, sensibly trying to avoid whatever might confuse him. But sometimes a word burst in his mouth, and what a revolution, what a dream of things then welled up out of such a cold, burned-out double word as tree kitten or rose lips!

Sitting on that plank in his cell that was both his bed and his table, he deplored his education, which had not taught him to express himself properly. The little creature with her mouse eyes who was still making so much trouble for him, even though she'd been underground for some time, made him angry. They were all on her side. He lumbered to his feet. He felt fragile, like charred wood. He was hungry again; the prison fare fell far short of satisfying a huge man like him, and he had no money for better. In such a state it was impossible for him to think of everything they wanted to know. One of these changes had come on, for days and weeks, the way March comes, or April, and then this business had happened. He knew nothing more about it than the police already had in their files; he didn't even know how it had got into their files. The reasons, the considerations he could remember, he had already stated in court anyway. But what had really happened seemed to him as if he had suddenly said fluently in a foreign language something that made him feel good but that he could no longer repeat.

"I just want it over and done with as soon as possible!" Moosbrugger thought.

∞

Legally, Moosbrugger's case could be summed up in a sentence. He was one of those borderline cases in law and forensic medicine known even to the layman as a case of diminished responsibility.

These unfortunates typically suffer not only substandard health but also have a substandard disease. Nature has a peculiar preference for producing such people in droves. *Natura non fecit saltus,* she makes no jumps but prefers gradual transitions; even on the grand scale she keeps the world in a transitional state between imbecility and sanity. But the law takes no notice of this. It says: *Non datur tertium sive medium inter duo contradictoria,* or in plain language, a person is either capable or not capable of breaking the law; between two contraries there is no third or middle state. It is this ability to choose that makes a person liable to punishment. His liability to punishment makes him legally a person, and as a person in the legal sense he shares in the suprapersonal benefaction of the law. Anyone who cannot grasp this right away should think of the cavalry. A horse that goes berserk every time someone attempts to mount it is treated with special care, given the softest bandages, the best riders, the choicest fodder, and the most patient handling. But if a cavalryman is guilty of some lapse, he is put in irons, locked in a flea-ridden cage, and deprived of his rations. The reasoning behind this difference is that the horse belongs merely to the empirical animal kingdom, while the dragoon belongs to the logical and moral kingdom. So understood, a person is distinguished from the animals—and, one may add, from the insane—in that he is capable, according to his intellectual and moral faculties, of acting against the law and of committing a crime. Since a person's liability to punishment is the quality that elevates him to the status of a moral being in the first place, it is understandable that the pillars of the law grimly hang on to it.

There is also the unfortunate complication that court psychiatrists, who would be called upon to oppose this situation, are usually far more timid professionally than the jurists. They certify as really insane only those persons they cannot cure—which is a modest exaggeration, since they cannot cure the others either. They distinguish between incurable mental diseases, the kind that with God's help will improve after a while of their own accord, and the kind that the doctor cannot cure either but that the patient could have avoided, assuming of course that the right influences and considerations had providentially been brought to bear on him in time. These second and third groups supply those lesser patients whom the angel of medicine treats as sick people when they come to him in his private practice, but whom he shyly leaves to the angel of law when he encounters them in his forensic practice.

Such a case was Moosbrugger. In the course of his life, respectable enough except when interrupted by those unaccountable fits of bloodthirstiness, he had as often been confined in mental institutions as he had been let go, and had been variously diagnosed as a paralytic, paranoiac, epileptic, and manic-depressive psychotic, until at his recent trial two particularly conscientious forensic psychiatrists had restored his sanity to him. Of course, there was not a single person in that vast crowded courtroom, the doctors included, who was not convinced that Moosbrugger was insane, one way or another;

but it was not a way that corresponded to the conditions of insanity laid down by the law, so this insanity could not be acknowledged by conscientious minds. For if one is partly insane, one is also, juridically, partly sane, and if one is partly sane one is at least partly responsible for one's actions, and if one is partly responsible one is wholly responsible; for responsibility is, as they say, that state in which the individual has the power to devote himself to a specific purpose of his own free will, independently of any compelling necessity, and one cannot simultaneously possess and lack such self-determination.

Not that this excludes the existence of persons whose circumstances and predispositions make it hard for them to "resist immoral impulses" and "opt for the good," as the lawyers put it, and Moosbrugger was such a person, in whom circumstances that would have no effect at all on others were enough to trigger the "intent" to commit an offense. First, however, his powers of reasoning and judgment were sufficiently intact, in the view of the court, so that an effort on his part could just as well have left the crime uncommitted, and there was no reason to exclude him from the moral estate of responsibility. Second, a well-ordered judicial system demands that every culpable act that is wittingly and willingly performed be punished. And third, judicial logic assumes that in all insane persons—with the exception of the most unfortunate, who when asked to multiply seven times seven stick out their tongue, or answer "Me" when asked to name His Imperial and Royal Majesty—there is still present a minimal power of discrimination and self-control and that it would only have taken a special effort of intelligence and willpower to recognize the criminal nature of the deed and to resist the criminal impulses. It is surely the least one has a right to expect from such dangerous persons!

Law courts resemble wine cellars in which the wisdom of our forefathers lies in bottles. One opens them and could weep at how unpalatable the highest, most effervescent, degree of the human striving for precision can be before it reaches perfection. And yet it seems to intoxicate the insufficiently seasoned mind.

It is a well-known phenomenon that the angel of medicine, if he has listened too long to lawyers' arguments, too often forgets his own mission. He then folds his wings with a clatter and conducts himself in court like a reserve angel of law.

Meanwhile Moosbrugger was still sitting in a detention cell at the district courthouse while his case was under study. His counsel had got fresh wind in his sails and was using delaying tactics with the authorities to keep the case from coming to a final conclusion.

Moosbrugger smiled at all this. He smiled from boredom.

Boredom rocked his mind like a cradle. Ordinarily boredom blots out the mind, but his was rocked by it, this time anyway. He felt like an actor in his dressing room, waiting for his cue.

If Moosbrugger had had a big sword, he'd have drawn it and chopped the head off his chair. He would have chopped the head off the table and the window, the slop bucket, the door. Then he would have set his own head on everything, because in this cell there was only one head, his own, and that was as it should be. He could imagine his head sitting on top of things, with its broad skull, its hair like a fur cap pulled down over his forehead; he liked that.

If only the room were bigger and the food better!

He was quite glad not to see people. People were hard to take. They often had a way of spitting, or of hunching up a shoulder, that made a man feel down in the mouth and ready to drive a fist through their back, like punching a hole in the wall. Moosbrugger did not believe in God, only in what he could figure out for himself. His contemptuous terms for the eternal truths were: the cop, the bench, the preacher. He knew he could count on no one but himself to take care of things, and such a man sometimes feels that others are there only to get in his way. He saw what he had seen so often: the inkstands, the green baize, the pencils, the Emperor's portrait on the wall, the way they all sat there around him: a booby trap camouflaged, not with grass and green leaves, just with the feeling: That's how it is. Then remembered things would pop into his head—the way a bush stood at the river bend, the creak of a pump handle, bits of different landscapes all jumbled up, an endless stock of memories of things he hadn't realized he'd noticed at the time. "I bet I could tell them a thing or two," he thought. He was day-dreaming like a youngster: a man they had locked up so often he never grew older. "Next time I'll have to take a closer look at it," Moosbrugger thought, "otherwise they'll never understand." Then he smiled sternly and spoke to the judges about himself, like a father saying about his son: "Just you lock him up, that good-for-nothing, he needs to be taught a lesson."

Sometimes he felt annoyed, of course, with the prison regulations. Or he was hurting somewhere. But then he could ask to see the prison doctor or the warden, and things fell into place again, like water closing over a dead rat that had fallen in. Not that he thought of it quite in these terms, but he kept having the sense almost constantly these days, even if he did not have the words for it, that he was like a great shining sheet of water, not to be disturbed by anything.

The words he did have were: hm-hm, uh-uh.

The table was Moosbrugger.

The chair was Moosbrugger.

The barred window and the bolted door were himself.

There was nothing at all crazy or out of the ordinary in what he meant. It was just that the rubber bands were gone. Behind every thing or creature, when it tries to get really close to another, is a rubber band, pulling. Otherwise, things might finally go right through one another. Every movement is reined in by a rubber band that won't let a person do quite what he wants. Now, suddenly, all those rubber bands were gone. Or was it just the feeling of being held in check, as if by rubber bands?

Maybe one just can't cut it so fine? "For instance, women keep their stockings up with elastic. There it is!" Moosbrugger thought. "They wear garters on their legs like amulets. Under their skirts. Just like the rings they paint around fruit trees to stop the worms from crawling up."

But we mention this only in passing. Lest anyone suppose that Moosbrugger felt he had to stay on good terms with everything. It wasn't really like that. It was only that he was both inside and outside.

He was the boss now, and he acted bossy. He was putting things in order before they killed him off. The moment he thought of anything, anything he pleased, it obeyed him like a well-trained dog to whom you say: "Down, boy!" Locked up though he was, he had a tremendous sense of power.

On the dot, his soup was brought. On the dot, he was awakened and taken out for his walk. Everything in his cell was on the mark, strict and immovable. This sometimes seemed incredible to him. He had the strangely topsy-turvy impression that all this order emanated from him, even though he knew that it was being imposed on him.

Other people have this sort of experience when they are stretched out in the summery shade of a hedge, the bees are buzzing, and the sun rides small and hard in the milky sky: the world revolves around them like a mechanical toy. Moosbrugger felt it when he merely looked at the geometric scene presented by his cell.

At such times he noticed that he had a mad craving for good food; he dreamed of it, and by day the outlines of a good plate of roast pork kept rising up before his eyes with an uncanny persistence the moment his mind turned back from other preoccupations. "Two portions!" Moosbrugger then ordered. "No, make it three!" He thought this so hard, and heaped up his imaginary plate so greedily, that he instantly felt full to bursting, to the point of nausea; he gorged himself in his imagination. "Why," he wondered, wagging his head, "why do I feel so stuffed, so soon after wanting to eat? Between eating and bursting lie all the pleasures of this world! Hell, what a world! There are hundreds of examples to prove how little space it gives you. To take just one, for instance: a woman you don't have is like

the moon at night climbing higher and higher, sucking and sucking at your heart; but once you've had her, you feel like
trampling on her face with your boots. Why is it like that?" He
remembered being asked about it lots of times. One could
answer: Women are women *and* men too, because men chase
after them. But it was only one more thing that the people who
asked all the questions wouldn't really understand. So they
asked him why he thought that people were in cahoots against
him. As if even his own body wasn't in cahoots with them! This
was quite obvious where women were concerned, of course, but
even with men his body understood things better than he did
himself. One word leads to another, you know what's what,
you're in each other's pocket all day long, and then, in a flash,
you've somehow crossed that narrow borderline where you get
along with them without any trouble. But if his body had got
him into this, it had better get him out of it again! All
Moosbrugger could remember was that he'd been vexed or
frightened, and his chest with its arms flailing had rushed at
them like a big dog on command. That was all Moosbrugger
could understand anyway; between getting along and being fed
up there's only a thin line, that's all, and once something gets
started it soon gets scary and tight.

Those people who were always using those foreign words and
were always sitting in judgment on him would keep throwing
this up to him: "But you don't go and kill a man just for that,
surely!" Moosbrugger only shrugged. People have been done in
for a few pennies, or for nothing at all, when someone happened
to feel like it. But he had more self-respect than that, he wasn't
one of that kind. In time the rebuke registered with him; he
found himself wondering why he felt the world closing in on
him, or whatever you might call it, time and again, so that he
had to clear a space for himself by force, in order that the blood
could drain out of his head again. He thought it over. But
wasn't it just the same with thinking too? Whenever he felt in
the right mood for doing some thinking, the pleasure of it made
him want to smile. Then his thoughts stopped itching under the

skull, and suddenly there was just one idea there. It was like the difference between an infant's toddling along and a fine figure of a woman dancing. It was like being under a spell. There's the sound of an accordion being played, a lamp stands on the table, butterflies come inside, out of the summer night—that was how his thoughts came fluttering into the light of the one idea, or else Moosbrugger grabbed them with his big fingers as they came and crushed them, looking for one breathtaking moment like little dragons caught there. A drop of Moosbrugger's blood had fallen into the world. You couldn't see it because it was dark, but he could feel what was going on out there. The tangled mess smoothed itself out. A soundless dance replaced the intolerable buzzing with which the world so often tormented him. Everything that happened was lovely now, just as a homely girl can be lovely when she no longer stands alone but is taken by the hand and whirled around in a dance, her face turned upward to a staircase from which others are looking down at her. It was a strange business. When Moosbrugger opened his eyes and looked at the people who happened to be nearby at such a moment, when everything was dancing to his tune, as it were, they, too, seemed lovely to him. They were no longer in league against him, they did not form a wall against him, and he realized that it was only the strain of getting the better of him that twisted the look of people and things like some crushing weight. At such times Moosbrugger danced for them. He danced with dignity and invisibly, he who never danced with anyone in real life, moved by a music that increasingly turned into self-communion and sleep, the womb of the Mother of God, and finally the peace of God himself, a wondrously incredible state of deathlike release; he danced for days, unseen by anyone, until it was all outside, all out of him, clinging to things around him like a cobweb stiffened and made useless by the frost.

How could anyone who had never been through all this judge the rest? After those days and weeks when Moosbrugger felt so light he could almost slip out of his skin, there always came those long stretches of imprisonment. The public prisons were nothing by comparison. Then when he tried to think, everything inside him shriveled up, bitter and empty. He hated the workingmen's study centers and the night schools where they tried to tell him how to think—after all, he knew the heady feeling of his thoughts taking off with long strides, as if on stilts! They made him feel as if he had to drag himself through the world on leaden feet, hoping to find some place where things might be different again.

Now he thought back to that hope with no more than a pitying smile. He had never managed to find a possible resting point midway between his two extremes. He was fed up. He smiled grandly at oncoming death.

He had, after all, seen quite a bit of the world. Bavaria and Austria, all the way to Turkey. And a great deal had happened during his lifetime that he had read about in the papers. An eventful time, on the whole. Deep down he was quite proud to have been a part of it all. Thinking it over bit by bit, he had to take it as a troubled and dreary business, but his own track did run right across it; looking back, you could see it clearly, from birth to death. Moosbrugger was far from feeling that he would actually be executed; he was executing himself, with the help of those other people, that was the way he looked at what was coming. It all added up to a whole, of sorts: the highways, the towns, the cops and the birds, the dead and his own death. It wasn't altogether clear to him, and the others understood it even less, though they could talk more glibly about it.

He spat and thought of the sky, which looks like a mousetrap covered in blue. "The kind they make in Slovakia, those round, high mousetraps," he thought.

∞

Moosbrugger was still in prison, waiting for further psychiatric examinations. It felt like a solid stack of days. Each day made itself distinctly felt when it came, of course, but toward evening it already began to merge with the stack. Moosbrugger certainly registered the presence of convicts, guards, corridors, court-yards, a glimpse of blue sky, a passing cloud or two, food, water, and now and then an official checking up on him, but these impressions were too feeble to be lasting. He had no watch, no sun, no work, to tell him the time. He was always hungry. He was always tired, from pacing around his seven square yards, which is far more tiring than wandering freely for miles. He was bored with everything he did, as if he had to keep stirring a pot of glue. But when he considered it as a whole, it seemed to him that day and night, his cleaning his plate and again cleaning his plate, inspections and checkups, all droned along one after the other without a break, and he found that entertaining. His life clock had gone out of order; it could be turned ahead or back. He liked that; it was his sort of thing. Things long past and fresh happenings were no longer kept apart artificially, and when it was all the same, then what they called "at different times" no longer stuck to it like the red thread they tie to a twin baby's neck so they can tell it from the other one. All the irrelevancies vanished from his life. When he pondered this life of his, he talked with himself inwardly, slowly, laying equal stress on every syllable; in this way life sang a different tune from the one heard every day. He often let his mind linger on a word for a long time, and when he finally moved on, without quite knowing how, after a while the word would turn up again somewhere else. It tickled him to think how much was happening for him that nobody knew about. The sense of being inwardly at peace with himself that sometimes came to him is hard to describe. Anyone can conceive of a man's life flowing along like a brook, but what Moosbrugger felt was his life flowing like a brook through a vast, still lake. As it flowed onward it continued to mingle with what it was leaving behind and became almost indistinguishable from the movements on either side of it. Once, in a half-waking dream, he had a sense of having worn this life's Moosbrugger like an ill-fitting coat on his back; now, when he opened it a bit, the most curious sort of lining came billowing out silkily, endless as a forest.

He no longer cared what was going on outside. Somewhere a war was going on. Somewhere there was a big wedding. Now the King of Belukhastan is coming, he thought. Everywhere soldiers were being drilled, whores were walking their beat, carpenters were standing among rafters. In the taverns of Stuttgart the beer came pouring from the same curving yellow taps as in Belgrade. On the road there were always the police demanding to see your papers. Then they stamped them. Everywhere there are bedbugs or no bedbugs. Work or no work. The women are the same everywhere. The doctors in all the hospitals are the same. When a man leaves his work in the evening the streets are full of people with nothing to do. It's all the same, always and everywhere; nobody has any new ideas. When Moosbrugger saw his first plane overhead in the blue sky—now, that was something! But then there was one plane after another, and they all looked alike. The sameness of things out there was different from the way his thoughts were all alike in being wonderful. He couldn't figure it out, and anyway it had always got in his way. He shook his head. To hell with the world, he thought. Or to hell with him and let them hang him: whatever happened, what did he have to lose . . . ?

And yet he sometimes would walk as if absentmindedly to the door and quietly try the place where the lock was on the outside. Then an eye would glare through the peephole and an angry voice come from the corridor, calling him names. Such insults made Moosbrugger move quickly back into his cell, and it was then that he felt locked up and robbed. Four walls and an iron door are nothing when you can freely walk in and out. Bars on an unfamiliar window are nothing special, and a plank bed or wooden table always in its place is quite in order. It's only when a man can't do what he wants with them that something crazy happens. Here things, made by human beings to serve them, slaves whose appearance one doesn't even bother to notice, suddenly get uppity. They block one's way. When Moosbrugger noticed these things giving him orders he had a good mind to smash them, and it was a struggle to convince himself that it was beneath him to fight these minions of the law. But his hands were twitching so hard he was afraid he was going to have a fit.

Out of the whole wide world they had picked these seven square yards, and Moosbrugger was pacing them, back and forth. The minds of the sane people out there, incidentally, who were not locked up, worked much the same as his own. They who had taken such a lively interest in him not so long ago had quickly forgotten him. He had been put in this place like a nail driven into the wall; once in, nobody notices it anymore. Other Moosbruggers were taking their turn; they were not himself, not even the same person every time, but they served the same purpose. There had been a sex crime, a grim story, a horrible murder, the act of a madman, of a man not quite responsible, the sort of thing to watch out for, but then the police and the courts had done their job. . . . Such vague and vacuous generalizations and memory tags loosely held the now-desiccated remains of the incident somewhere in their wide net. Moosbrugger's name was forgotten, the details were forgotten. He might have been "a squirrel, a hare, or a fox," the public remembered nothing specific about him, there remained only dim, wide areas of overlapping general notions, like the gray shimmer in a telescope focused at too great a distance. This failure to make connections, the cruelty of a mind that shuffles concepts around without bothering about the burden of suffering and life that weighs down every decision, was what the general mind had in common with that of Moosbrugger; but what was in his crazed brain a dream, a fairy tale, that flawed or odd spot in the mirror of consciousness which does not reflect reality but lets the light through, was lacking in society as a whole, unless some individual, in his obscure excitement, showed a hint of it here and there.

And what did concern Moosbrugger specifically, this particular Moosbrugger and none other, the one temporarily stored on these seven square yards of the world—the feeding, surveillance, authorized treatment, final disposal of the case by life or death sentence—was all in the hands of a relatively small group of people with a wholly different attitude. Here eyes on duty spied on him, voices came down hard on him for the slightest misstep. Never did fewer than two guards enter his cell. He was always handcuffed when they took him through the corridors. They acted with the fear and caution that had to do with this particular Moosbrugger within this limited area but was in strange contrast with the treatment accorded to him in general. He often complained about these strict measures. But when he did, the captain, the warden, the doctor, the priest, whoever heard him, turned a frozen face on him and told him he was being treated according to regulations. So regulations had taken the place of the interest the world had once taken in him, and Moosbrugger thought: "You've got a long rope around your neck and you can't see who's pulling it." He was roped to the outside world but, as it were, around the corner, out of sight. People who mostly never gave him a thought, who did not even know he existed, or to whom he meant at best no more than what some chicken on a village street means to a university professor of zoology—they were all in it together, preparing the doom that he felt tugging at him in some ghostly way. Some skirt in an office was typing a memo for his record. A registrar was ingeniously classifying it for filing. Some high functionary of the court was drawing up the latest directive for implementing his sentence. Psychiatrists were debating how to draw the line between the purely psychopathic constitution in certain cases of epilepsy and its manifestations when combined with other syndromes. Jurists were analyzing the factors that mitigated culpability in relation to factors that might modify the sentence. A bishop denounced the unraveling of the moral fabric, and a game warden's complaint to Bonadea's husband, the judge, about the excessive increase in foxes was reinforcing that eminent legal mind's bias in favor of reinforcing the inflexibility of the law.

It is such impersonal matters that go into the making of personal happenings in a way that for the present eludes description. When Moosbrugger's case was shorn of all its individual romantic elements, of interest only to him and to the few people he had murdered, not much more was left of it than what could be gathered from the list of references to works cited that Ulrich's father had enclosed in a recent letter to his son. Such a list looks like this: AH. AMP. AAC. AKA. AP. ASZ. BKL. BGK. BUD. CN. DTJ. DJZ. FBvM. GA. GS. JKV. KBSA. MMW. NG. PNW. R. VSvM. WMW. ZGS. ZMB. ZP. ZSS. Addickes ibid. Beling ibid., and so on. Written out, these would read: Annales d'Hygiène Publique et de Médecine légale, ed. Brouardel, Paris; Annales Médico-Psychologiques, ed. Ritti . . . etc., etc., making a list a page long even when reduced to the briefest of abbreviations. The truth is not a crystal that can be slipped into one's pocket, but an endless current into which one falls headlong. Imagine every one of these abbreviations trailing a dozen or hundreds of printed pages, for each page a man with ten fingers writing it, and for each of his ten fingers ten disciples and ten opponents with ten fingers each, and at every fingertip a tenth of a personal idea, and you have a dim notion of what the truth is like. Without it not even that well-known sparrow can fall off the roof. Sun, wind, food brought it there, and illness, hunger, cold, or a cat killed it, but none of this could have happened without the operation of laws, biological, psychological, meteorological, physical, chemical, sociological, and all the rest, and it is much less of a strain to be merely looking for such laws than to have to make them up, as is done in the moral and judicial disciplines.

As for Moosbrugger himself, with his great respect for human knowledge, although he had, unfortunately, so small a portion of it: he never would have understood his situation completely even had he known exactly what it was. He had a dim sense of it. He felt that he was in an unstable condition. His big, powerful body was not as solid as it looked. Sometimes the open sky peered right into his skull. Just as it had, so often, in the old days on the road. And though he sometimes wished he could shake it off, he was never free, these days, of a certain solemn exaltation that streamed toward him, through the prison walls, from all the world. So there he sat, the wild, captive threat of a dreaded act, like an uninhabited coral island in a boundless sea of scientific papers that surrounded him invisibly on all sides. ∿

INTERPRETIVE QUESTIONS
FOR DISCUSSION

Why does Moosbrugger murder the prostitute who accosts him and begs him to take her home with him?

1. Why does Moosbrugger insist that he could not possibly be a sex murderer because women inspire only feelings of aversion in him? (81)

2. Why does the author suggest that Moosbrugger's treatment of women is like the playful violence of a dog or a cat? Why do the women Moosbrugger encounters form "processions," even when they have nothing to do with each other? (81)

3. Why does Moosbrugger think that women are "in the forefront of the conspiracy against him"? (83)

4. Why does Moosbrugger think that in walking away from the prostitute he is "drawing her after him"? Why does he think that "that creature, trailing him, was himself again"—a "second self"? (84–85)

5. Why does Moosbrugger feel he has to keep stabbing the prostitute, even after she has fallen, "until he had completely separated her from himself"? (85)

6. Why does Moosbrugger leave the corpse where it can be "more easily found and buried . . . because now it was no longer her fault"? (85–86)

7. Why does Moosbrugger blame the woman he has killed for having gotten him "into this mess"? Why does she seem to him "a crude, nasty bitch contrasted with a child, if he compared her to himself"? (98)

8. Why does Moosbrugger attack his master's wife when she rejects his advances? (99–100)

9. Why does Moosbrugger feel an overwhelming temptation to "go for his knife" when he is unable "to hold the world together"? (104)

10. Why does Moosbrugger feel "the world closing in on him . . . time and again, so that he had to clear a space for himself by force"? (111)

Suggested textual analysis
Pages 84–86: beginning, "And so the end of that night had come," and ending, "it was no longer her fault."

Are we meant to agree with Moosbrugger that he has been "cheated of his justice"?

1. Why are the reporters reluctant to "banish" Moosbrugger "from their own world into the world of the insane"? Why are people more preoccupied with his crime than with their own life's work? (78–79)

2. Why does Moosbrugger not deny what he has done, but simply want his deeds "understood as the mishaps of an important philosophy of life"? (83)

3. Why does Moosbrugger cry "Bravo!" at the prosecutor's argument that he is a public menace and give out good marks to witnesses who testify to his sanity? Why can't he understand how he is working himself "one level deeper into his guilt"? (86)

4. Why does Moosbrugger say, "I . . . have achieved my purpose," when he is judged responsible for his actions, and then after being read the death sentence say, "I must confess to you that you have condemned a madman"? (88)

5. Why does Moosbrugger's story cause Ulrich to be preoccupied with "the awful way society had of toying with its victims"? (93)

6. Why are we told that though mankind will kill Moosbrugger, it "still has the weakness to venerate those men who might—who knows?—have acquitted him"? (94)

7. Why does Moosbrugger agree to confess when the police superintendent says, "I beseech you: grant me success!"? (96)

8. Why are we told that Moosbrugger's insanity "could not be acknowledged by conscientious minds"? (107)

9. Why are we told that it is "impersonal matters" that go into the making of "personal happenings" such as Moosbrugger's death sentence? (117–118)

10. Why is Moosbrugger unable to gain clemency for his crime, even though everyone involved in his trial is convinced that he is "insane, one way or another"? (106)

Suggested textual analyses

Pages 77–80: from the beginning of the selection to "even if it faded a little when his attention wandered."

Pages 105–108: beginning, "Legally, Moosbrugger's case," and ending, "like a reserve angel of law."

Why does Ulrich think that Moosbrugger's madness is "no more than a distortion of our own elements of being"—that "if mankind could dream as a whole, that dream would be Moosbrugger"?

1. Why are we told that "the more important things take place today in the abstract, and the more trivial ones in real life"? Why is the case of Moosbrugger not something that takes place "in real life"? (79)

2. Why can't Moosbrugger bear to be called insane? (80, 102)

3. Why does Moosbrugger regard his pathological nature as "a stronger and higher sense of his own self"? (82)

4. Why does Moosbrugger see his criminal acts as having "perched on him like birds that had flown in from somewhere or other"? (87)

5. Why are we told that nature has a "peculiar preference" for producing borderline cases—for keeping the world "in a transitional state between imbecility and sanity"? (105)

6. Why does Moosbrugger alternate between the inability to speak and the inability to stop the voices inside his head? Why does he experience the latter periods as "all meaning"? (101–102)

7. Why does Moosbrugger sometimes feel that the rubber bands separating him from everything else have disappeared? (109)

8. Why does a "soundless dance" sometimes replace in Moosbrugger's mind "the intolerable buzzing with which the world so often tormented him"? (112)

9. Why, when he reflects on his life, does Moosbrugger think that "it all added up to a whole, of sorts: the highways, the towns, the cops and the birds, the dead and his own death"? Why does he feel he is "executing himself"? (113)

10. Why are we told that in its disregard for Moosbrugger the general public shares with him "the cruelty of a mind that shuffles concepts around without bothering about the burden of suffering and life that weighs down every decision"? (116)

Suggested textual analyses

Pages 101–104: beginning, "This was the real beginning of the time they all wanted to know about," and ending, "to hold the world together."

Pages 109–112: beginning, "There was nothing at all crazy," and ending, "like a cobweb stiffened and made useless by the frost."

FOR FURTHER REFLECTION

1. Why are we fascinated with horrible crimes and the people who commit them?

2. Where do you draw the line between guilty and not guilty in a case of "diminished responsibility" like Moosbrugger's?

3. Does televising trials such as Moosbrugger's make them more, or less, real and humane to us?

4. Is there a Moosbrugger in all of us? If humanity could dream as a whole, would that dream be Moosbrugger?

5. Do you agree that it is "liability to punishment" that elevates a person to the status of a moral being?

6. Do you agree with Ulrich that the truth is not a crystal that can be slipped into one's pocket, but an endless current into which one falls headlong?

THE SORCERER'S
APPRENTICE

Charles Johnson

CHARLES JOHNSON (1948–) was born in Evanston, Illinois. A scholar and critic as well as an author of fiction, Johnson explores in his writing how African Americans have used and transformed philosophical traditions. His novel *Middle Passage,* about the slave trade between West Africa and the Americas, was a bestseller and critical success, and in 1990 Johnson became only the second African American man to win the National Book Award. His collection of stories, *The Sorcerer's Apprentice: Tales and Conjurations,* was nominated for the PEN/Faulkner Award for fiction in 1988.

THERE WAS A TIME, long ago, when many sorcerers lived in South Carolina, men not long from slavery who remembered the white magic of the Ekpe cults and Cameroons, and by far the greatest of these wizards was a blacksmith named Rubin Bailey. Believing he was old, and would soon die, the Sorcerer decided to pass his learning along to an apprentice. From a family near Abbeville he selected a boy, Allan, whose father, Richard Jackson, Rubin once healed after an accident, and for this Allan loved the Sorcerer, especially the effects of his craft, which comforted the sick, held back evil, and blighted the enemies of newly freed slaves with locusts and bad health. "My house," Richard told the wizard, "has been honored." His son swore to serve his teacher faithfully, then those who looked to the Sorcerer, in all ways. With his father's blessing, the boy moved his belongings into the Sorcerer's home, a houseboat covered with strips of scrap metal, on the river.

But Rubin Bailey's first teachings seemed to Allan to be no teachings at all. "Bring in fresh water," Rubin told his apprentice. "Scrape barnacles off the boat." He never spoke of sorcery. Around the boy he tied his blacksmith's apron, and guided his hand in hammering out the horseshoes Rubin sold in town, but not once in the first month did Rubin pass along the recipes for magic. Patiently, Allan performed these duties in perfect submission to the Sorcerer, for it seemed rude to express displeasure to a man he wished to emulate, but his heart knocked for the higher knowledge, the techniques that would, he hoped, work miracles.

At last, as they finished a meal of boiled pork and collards one evening, he complained bitterly: "You haven't told me anything yet!" Allan regretted this outburst immediately, and lowered his head. "Have I done wrong?"

For a moment the Sorcerer was silent. He spiced his coffee with rum, dipped in his bread, chewed slowly, then looked up, steadily, at the boy. "You are the best of students. And you wish to do good, but you can't be too faithful, or too eager, or the good becomes evil."

"Now I don't understand." Allan said. "By themselves the tricks aren't good *or* evil, and if you plan to do good, then the results must be good."

Rubin exhaled, finished his coffee, then shoved his plate toward the boy. "Clean the dishes," he said. Then, more gently: "What I know has worked I will teach. There is no certainty these things can work for you, or even for me, a second time. White magic comes and goes. I'm teaching you a trade, Allan. You will never starve. This is because after fifty years, I still can't foresee if an incantation will be magic or foolishness."

These were not, of course, the answers Allan longed to hear. He said, "Yes, sir," and quietly cleared away their dishes. If he had replied aloud to Rubin, as he did silently while toweling dry their silverware later that night, he would have told the Sorcerer, "You are the greatest magician in the world because you have studied magic and the long-dead masters of magic, and I believe, even if you do not, that the secret of doing good is a good heart and having a hundred spells at your disposal, so I will study everything—the words and timbre and tone of your voice as you conjure, and listen to those you have heard. Then I, too, will have magic and can do good." He washed his underwear in the moonlight, as is fitting for a fledgling magician, tossed his dishpan water into the river, and, after hanging his wash-pail on a hook behind Rubin's front door, undressed, and fell asleep with these thoughts: To do good is a very great thing, the *only* thing, but a magician must be able to conjure at a moment's notice. Surely it is all a question of know-how.

So it was that after a few months the Sorcerer's apprentice learned well and quickly when Rubin Bailey finally began to teach. In Allan's growth was the greatest joy. Each spell he showed proudly to his father and Richard's friends when he traveled home once a year. Unbeknownst to the Sorcerer, he held simple exhibits for their entertainment—harmless prestidigitation like throwing his voice or levitating logs stacked by the toolshed. However pleased Richard might have been, he gave no sign. Allan's father never joked or laughed too loudly. He was the sort of man who held his feelings in, and people took this for strength. Allan's mother, Beatrice, a tall, thick-waisted woman, had told him (for Richard would not) how when she was carrying Allan, they rode a hay wagon to a scrub-ball in Abbeville on Freedom Day. Richard fell beneath the wagon. A wheel smashed his thumb open to the bone. "Somebody better go for Rubin Bailey," was all Richard said, and he stared like it might be a stranger's hand. And Allan remembered Richard toiling so long in the sun he couldn't eat some evenings unless he first emptied his stomach by forcing himself to vomit. His father squirreled away money in their mattresses, saving for seven years to buy the land they worked. When he had $600—half what they needed—he grew afraid of theft, so Beatrice took their money to one of the banks in town. She stood in line behind a northern-looking Negro who said his name was Grady Armstrong. "I work for the bank across the street," he told Beatrice. "You wouldn't be interested in part-time work, would you? We need a woman to clean, someone reliable, but she has to keep her savings with us." Didn't they need the money? Beatrice would ask Allan, later, when Richard left them alone at night. Wouldn't the extra work help her husband? She followed Grady Armstrong, whose easy, loose-hinged walk led them to the second bank across the street. "Have you ever deposited money before?" asked Grady. "No," she said. Taking her envelope, he said, "Then I'll do it for you." On the boardwalk, Beatrice waited. And waited. After five minutes, she opened the door, found no Grady Armstrong, and flew screaming the fifteen miles back to the fields and Richard, who listened and chewed his lip, but said nothing. He leaned, Allan remembered, in the farmhouse door, smoking his cigars and watching only Lord knew what in the darkness—exactly as he stood the following year, when Beatrice, after swallowing rat poison, passed on.

Allan supposed it was risky to feel if you had grown up, like Richard, in a world of nightriders. There was too much to lose. Any attachment ended in separation, grief. If once you let yourself care, the crying might never stop. So he assumed his father was pleased with his apprenticeship to Rubin, though hearing him say this would have meant the world to Allan. He did not mind that somehow the Sorcerer's personality seemed to permeate each spell like sweat staining fresh wood, because this, too, seemed to be the way of things. The magic was Rubin Bailey's, but when pressed, the Sorcerer confessed that the spells had been in circulation for centuries. They were a web of history and culture, like the king-sized quilts you saw as curiosities at country fairs, sewn by every woman in Abbeville, each having finished only a section, a single flower perhaps, so no man, strictly speaking, could own a mystic spell. "But when you kill a bird by pointing," crabbed Rubin from his rocking chair, "you don't *haveta* wave your left hand in the air and pinch your forefinger and thumb together like I do."

"Did I do that?" asked Allan.

Rubin hawked and spit over the side of the houseboat. "Every time."

"I just wanted to get it right." Looking at his hand, he felt ashamed—he was, after all, right-handed—then shoved it deep into his breeches. "The way you do it is so beautiful."

"I know." Rubin laughed. He reached into his coat, brought out his pipe, and looked for matches. Allan stepped inside, and the Sorcerer shouted behind him, "You shouldn't do it because my own teacher, who wore out fifteen flying carpets in his lifetime, told me it was wrong."

"Wrong?" The boy returned. He held a match close to the bowl of Rubin's pipe, cupping the flame. "Then why do you do it?"

"It works best for me that way, Allan. I have arthritis." He slanted his eyes left at his pupil. "Do you?"

The years passed, and Allan improved, even showing a certain flair, a style all his own that pleased Rubin, who praised the boy for his native talent, which did not come from knowledge and, it struck Allan, was wholly unreliable. When Esther Peters, a seamstress, broke her hip, it was not Rubin who the old woman called, but young Allan, who sat stiffly on a fiddle-back chair by her pallet, the fingers of his left hand spread over the bony ledge of her brow and rheumy eyes, whispering the rune that lifted her pain after Esther stopped asking, "Does he know what he doing, Rubin? This ain't how you did when I caught my hand in that cotton gin." Afterwards, as they walked the dark footpath leading back to the river, Rubin in front, the Sorcerer shared a fifth with the boy and paid him a terrifying compliment: "That was the best I've seen anybody do the spell for exorcism." He stroked his pupil's head. "God took *holt* of you back there—I don't see how you can do it that good again." The smile at the corners of Allan's mouth weighed a ton. He handed back Rubin's bottle, and said, "Me neither." The Sorcerer's flattery, if this was flattery, suspiciously resembled Halloween candy with hemlock inside. Allan could not speak to Rubin the rest of that night.

In the old days of sorcery, it often happened that pupils came to mistrust most their finest creations, those frighteningly effortless works that flew mysteriously from their lips when they weren't looking, and left the apprentice feeling, despite his pride, as baffled as his audience and afraid for his future—this was most true when the compliments compared a fledgling wizard to other magicians, as if the apprentice had achieved nothing new, or on his own. This is how Allan felt. The charm that cured Esther had whipped through him like wind through a reed pipe, or—more exactly, like music struggling to break free, liberate its volume and immensity from the confines of wood and brass. It made him feel unessential, anonymous, like a tool in which the spell sang itself, briefly borrowing his throat, then tossed him, Allan, aside when the miracle ended. To be so used was thrilling, but it gave the boy many bad nights. He lay half on his bed, half off. While Rubin slept, he yanked on his breeches and slipped outside. The river trembled with moonlight. Not far away, in a rowboat, a young man unbuttoned his lover. Allan heard their laughter and fought down the loneliness of a life devoted to discipline and sorcery. So many sacrifices. So many hours spent hunched over yellow, worm-holed scrolls. He pitched small pebbles into the water, and thought, If a conjurer cannot conjure at will, he is worthless. He must have knowledge, an armory of techniques, a thousand strategies, if he is to unfailingly do good. Toward this end the apprentice applied himself, often despising the spontaneity of his first achievement. He watched Rubin Bailey closely until on his fifth year on the river he had stayed by the Sorcerer too long and there was no more to learn.

"That can't be," said Allan. He was twenty-five, a full sorcerer himself by most standards, very handsome, more like his father now, at the height of his technical powers, with many honors and much brilliant thaumaturgy behind him, though none half as satisfying as his first exorcism rune for Esther Peters. He had, generally, the respect of everyone in Abbeville. And, it must be said, they waited eagerly for word of his first solo demonstration. This tortured Allan. He paced around the table, where Rubin sat repairing a fishing line. His belongings, rolled in a blanket, lay by the door. He pleaded, "There must be *one* more strategy."

"One more maybe," agreed the Sorcerer. "But what you need to know, you'll learn."

"Without you?" Allan shuddered. He saw himself, in a flash of probable futures, failing Rubin. Dishonoring Richard. Ridiculed by everyone. "How *can* I learn without you?"

"You just do like you did that evening when you helped Esther Peters. . . ."

That wasn't me, thought Allan. I was younger. I don't know how, but everything worked then. You were behind me. I've tried. I've tried the rain-making charm over and over. *It doesn't rain!* They're only words!

The old Sorcerer stood up and embraced Allan quickly, for he did not like sloppy good-byes or lingering glances or the silly things people said when they had to get across a room and out the door. "You go home and wait for your first caller. You'll do fine."

Allan followed his bare feet away from the houseboat, his head lowered and a light pain in his chest, a sort of flutter like a pigeon beating its wings over his heart—an old pain that first began when he suspected that pansophical knowledge counted for nothing. The apprentice said the spell for fair weather. Fifteen minutes later a light rain fell. He traipsed through mud into Abbeville, shoved his bag under an empty table in a tavern, and sat dripping in the shadows until he dried. A fat man pounded an off-key piano. Boot heels stamped the floor beneath Allan, who ordered tequila. He sucked lemon slices and drained off shot glasses. Gradually, liquor backwashed in his throat and the ache disappeared and his body felt transparent. Yet still he wondered: Was sorcery a gift given to a few, like poetry? Did the Lord come, lift you up, then drop you forever? If so, then he was finished, bottomed out, bellied up before he even began. He had not been born among the Allmuseri tribe in Africa, like Rubin, if this was necessary for magic. He had not come to New Orleans in a slave clipper, or been sold at the *cabildo*, if this was necessary. He had only, it seemed, a vast and painfully acquired yet hollow repertoire of tricks, and this meant he could be a parlor magician, which paid well enough, but he would never do good. If he could not help, what then? He knew no other trade. He had no other dignity. He had no other means to transform the world and no other influence upon men. His seventh tequila untasted, Allan squeezed the bridge of his nose with two fingers, rummaging through his mind for Rubin's phrase for the transmogrification of liquids into vapor. The demons of drunkenness (Saphathoral) and slow-thinking (Ruax) tangled his thoughts, but finally the words floated topside. Softly, he spoke the phrase, stunned at its beauty—at the Sorcerer's beauty, really— mumbling it under his breath so no one might hear, then opened his eyes on the soaking, square face of a man who wore a blue homespun shirt and butternut trousers, but had not been there an instant before: his father. Maybe he'd said the phrase for telekinesis. "Allan, I've been looking all over. How are you?"

"Like you see." His gaze dropped from his father to the full shot glass and he despaired.

"Are you sure you're all right? Your eyelids are puffy."

"I'm okay." He lifted the shot glass and made its contents vanish naturally. "I've had my last lesson."

"I know—I went looking for you on the river, and Rubin said you'd come home. Since I knew better, I came to Abbeville. There's a girl at the house wants to see you—Lizzie Harris. She was there when you sawed Deacon Wills in half." Richard picked up his son's bag. "She wants you to help her to—"

Allan shook his head violently. "Lizzie should see Rubin."

"She has." He reached for Allan's hat and placed it on his son's head. "He sent her to you. She's been waiting for hours."

Much rain fell upon Allan and his father, who walked as if his feet hurt, as they left town, but mainly it fell on Allan. His father's confidence in him was painful, his chatter about his son's promising future like the chronicle of someone else's life. This was the night that was bound to come. And now, he thought as they neared the tiny, hip-roofed farmhouse, swimming in fog, I shall fall from humiliation to impotency, from impotency to failure, from failure to death. He leaned weakly against the porch rail. His father scrambled ahead of him, though he was a big man built for endurance and not for speed, and stepped back to open the door for Allan. The Sorcerer's apprentice, stepping inside, decided quietly, definitely, without hope that if this solo flight failed, he would work upon himself the one spell Rubin had described but dared not demonstrate. If he could not help this girl Lizzie—and he feared he could not— he would go back to the river and bring forth demons—horrors that broke a man in half, ate his soul, then dragged him below the ground, where, Allan decided, those who could not do well the work of a magician belonged.

"Allan's here," his father said to someone in the sitting room. "My son is a Conjure Doctor, you know."

"I seen him," said a girl's voice. "Looks like he knows everything there is to know about magic."

The house, full of heirlooms, had changed little since Allan's last year with Rubin. The furniture was darkened by use. All the mirrors in his mother's bedroom were still covered by cloth. His father left week-old dishes on the hob, footswept his cigars under the bare, loose floorboards, and paint on the front porch had begun to peel in large strips. There in the sitting room, Lizzie Harris sat on Beatrice's old flat-bottomed roundabout. She was twice as big as Allan remembered her. Her loose dress and breast exposed as she fed her baby made, he supposed, the difference. Allan looked away while Lizzie drew her dress up, then reached into her bead purse for a shinplaster—Civil War currency—which she handed to him. "This is all you have?" He returned her money, pulled a milk stool beside her, and said, "Please, sit down." His hands were trembling. He needed to hold something to hide the shaking. Allan squeezed both his knees. "Now," he said, "what's wrong with the child?"

"Pearl don't eat," said Lizzie. "She hasn't touched food in two days, and the medicine Dr. Britton give her makes her spit. It's a simple thing," the girl assured him. "Make her eat."

He lifted the baby off Lizzie's lap, pulling the covering from her face. That she was beautiful made his hands shake even more. She kept her fists balled at her cheeks. Her eyes were light, bread-colored, but latticed by blood vessels. Allan said to his father, without facing him, "I think I need boiled Hound's Tongue and Sage. They're in my bag. Bring me the water from the herbs in a bowl." He hoisted the baby higher on his right arm and, holding the spoon of cold cereal in his left hand, praying silently, began a litany of every spell he knew to disperse suffering and the afflictions of the spirit. From his memory, where techniques lay stacked like crates in a storage bin, Allen unleashed a salvo of incantations. His father, standing nearby with a discolored spoon and the bowl, held his breath so long Allan could hear flies gently beating against the lamp glass of the lantern. Allan, using the spoon like a horseshoe, slipped the potion between her lips. "Eat, Pearl," the apprentice whispered. "Eat and live." Pearl spit up on his shirt. Allan closed his eyes and repeated slowly every syllable of every word of every spell in his possession. And ever he pushed the spoon of cereal against the child's teeth, ever she pushed it away, gagging, swinging her head, and wailing so Allan had to shout each word above her voice. He oozed sweat now. Wind changing direction outside shifted the pressure inside the room so suddenly that Allan's stomach turned violently—it was as if the farmhouse, snatched up a thousand feet, now hung in space. Pearl spit first clear fluids. Then blood. The apprentice attacked this mystery with a dazzling array of devices, analyzed it, looked at her with the critical, wrinkled brow of a philosopher, and mimed the Sorcerer so perfectly it seemed that Rubin, not Allan, worked magic in the room. But he was not Rubin Bailey. And the child suddenly stopped its struggle and relaxed in the apprentice's arms.

Lizzie yelped, "Why ain't Pearl crying?" He began repeating, futilely, his spells for the fifth time. Lizzie snatched his arm with such strength her fingers left blue spots on his skin. "That's enough!" she said. "You give her to me!"

"There's another way," Allan said, "another charm I've seen." But Lizzie Harris had reached the door. She threw a brusque "Good-bye" behind her to Richard and nothing to Allan. He knew they were back on the ground when Lizzie disappeared outside. Within the hour she would be at Rubin's houseboat. In two hours she would be at Esther Peters' home, broadcasting his failure.

"Allan," said Richard, stunned. "It didn't work."

"It's never worked." Allan put away the bowl, looked around the farmhouse for his bag, then a pail, and kissed his father's rough cheek. Startled, Richard pulled back sharply, as if he had stumbled sideways against the kiln. "I'm sorry," said Allan. It was not an easy thing to touch a man who so guarded, and for good reason, his emotions. "I'm not much of a Sorcerer, or blacksmith, or anything else."

"You're not going out this late, are you?" His father struggled, and Allan felt guilty for further confusing him with feeling. "Allan . . ."

His voice trailed off.

"There's one last spell I have to do." Allan touched his arm lightly, once, then drew back his hand. "Don't follow me, okay?"

On his way to the river Allan gathered the roots and stalks and stones he required to dredge up the demon kings. The sky was clear, the air dense, and the Devil was in it if he fouled even this conjuration. For now he was sure that white magic did not reside in ratiocination, education, or will. Skill was of no service. His talent was for pa(o)stiche.[1] He could imitate but never truly heal; impress but never conjure beauty; ape the good but never again give rise to a genuine spell. For that God or Creation, or the universe—it had several names—had to seize you, *use* you, as the Sorcerer said, because it needed a womb, shake you down, speak through you until the pain pearled into a beautiful spell that snapped the world back together. It had abandoned Allan, this possession. It had taken him, in a way,

---

1. [pastiche/postiche: pastiche—a blending of techniques; postiche—imitation or sham.]

like a lover, planted one pitiful seed, and said, " 'Bye now." This absence, this emptiness, this sterility he felt deep at his center. Beyond all doubt, he owed the universe far more than it owed him. To give was right; to ask wrong. From birth he was indebted to so many, like his father, and for so much. But you could not repay the universe, or anyone, or build a career as a Conjure Doctor on a single, brilliant spell. Talent, Allan saw, was a curse. To have served once—was this enough? Better perhaps never to have served at all than to go on, foolishly, in the wreckage of former grace, glossing over his frigidity with cheap fireworks, window dressing, a trashy display of pyrotechnics, gimmicks designed to distract others from seeing that the magician onstage was dead.

Now the Sorcerer's apprentice placed his stones and herbs into the pail, which he filled with river water; then he built a fire behind a rock. Rags of fog floated over the waste-clogged riverbank as Allan drew a horseshoe in chalk. He sat cross-legged in wet grass that smelled faintly of oil and fish, faced east, and cursed at the top of his voice. "I conjure and I invoke thee, O Magoa, strong king of the East. I order thee to obey me, to send thy servants Onoskelis and Tepheus."

Two froglike shapes stitched from the fumes of Allan's potion began to take form above the pail.

Next he invoked the demon king of the North, who brought Ornia, a beautiful, blue-skinned lamia from the river bottom. Her touch, Allan knew, was death. She wore a black gown, a necklace of dead spiders, and entered through the opening of the enchanted horseshoe. The South sent Rabdos, a griffinlike hound, all teeth and hair, that hurtled toward the apprentice from the woods; and from the West issued Bazazath, the most terrible of all—a collage of horns, cloven feet, and goatish eyes so wild Allan wrenched away his head. Upriver, he saw kerosene lamplight moving from the direction of town. A faraway voice called, "Allan? Allan? Allan, is that you? Allan, are you out there?" His father. The one he had truly harmed. Allan frowned and faced those he had summoned.

"Apprentice," rumbled Bazazath, "*student,* you risk your life by opening hell."

"I am only that, a student," said Allan, "the one who studies beauty, who wishes to give it back, but who cannot serve what he loves."

"You are wretched, indeed," said Bazazath, and he glanced back at the others. "Isn't he wretched?"

They said, as one, "Worse."

Allan did not understand. He felt Richard's presence hard by, heard him call from the mystic circle's edge, which no man or devil could break. "How am I worse?"

"Because," said the demon of the West, "to love the good, the beautiful is right, but to labor on and will the work when you are obviously *beneath* this service is to parody them, twist them beyond recognition, to lay hold of what was once beautiful and make it a monstrosity. It becomes *black* magic. Sorcery is relative, student—dialectical, if you like expensive speech. And this, exactly, is what you have done with the teachings of Rubin Bailey."

"No," blurted Allan.

The demon of the West smiled. "Yes."

"Then," Allan asked, "you must destroy me?" It was less a question than a request.

"That is why we are here." Bazazath opened his arms. "You must step closer."

He had not known before the real criminality of his deeds. How dreadful that love could disfigure the thing loved. Allan's eyes bent up toward Richard. It was too late for apologies. Too late for promises to improve. He had failed everyone, particularly his father, whose face now collapsed into tears, then hoarse weeping like some great animal with a broken spine. In a moment he would drop to both knees. Don't want me, thought Allan. Don't love me as I am. Could he do nothing right? His work caused irreparable harm—and his death, trivial as it was in his own eyes, that, too, would cause suffering. Why must his choices be so hard? If he returned home, his days would be a dreary marking time for magic, which might never come again, living to one side of what he had loved, and loved still, for fear of creating evil—this was surely the worst curse of all, waiting for grace, but in suicide he would drag his father's last treasure, dirtied as it was, into hell behind him.

"It grows late," said Bazazath. "Have you decided?"

The apprentice nodded, yes.

He scrubbed away part of the chalk circle with the ball of his foot, then stepped toward his father. The demons waited—two might still be had this night for the price of one. But Allan felt within his chest the first spring of resignation, a giving way of both the hunger to heal and the anxiety to avoid evil. Was this surrender the one thing the Sorcerer could not teach? His pupil did not know. Nor did he truly know, now that he was no longer a Sorcerer's apprentice with a bright future, how to comfort his father. Awkwardly, Allan lifted Richard's wrist with his right hand, for he was right-handed, then squeezed, tightly, the old man's thick, ruined fingers. For a second his father twitched back in an old slave reflex, the safety catch still on, then fell heavily toward his son. The demons looked on indifferently, then glanced at each other. After a moment they left, seeking better game. ∾

INTERPRETIVE QUESTIONS
FOR DISCUSSION

**Why does Rubin tell Allan that "the good becomes evil"
if the person performing the magic of healing is "too faithful,
or too eager"?**

1. Why does Allan long to become a sorcerer—a magician and healer who can "work miracles"? (130) Why is Allan obsessed with "unfailingly" doing good with his magic? (134)

2. Why does Allan think that "the secret of doing good is a good heart and having a hundred spells at your disposal"? (130)

3. Why is white magic described as being like "a web of history and culture, . . . so no man, strictly speaking, could own a mystic spell"? (132)

4. Why does Allan feel ashamed when Rubin points out that Allan performs spells using the same gestures that he uses?

5. After Allan cures Esther Peters, why does Rubin praise him by saying, "God took *holt* of you back there—I don't see how you can do it that good again"? (133)

6. Why does the magic that whipped through Allan to cure Esther Peters leave him feeling "unessential, anonymous"? (134)

7. Why does Rubin send Lizzie and her baby to Allan for a cure?

8. Why can Allan cure Esther Peters, who questions his ability, but not Lizzie's child at a time when he has earned everyone's confidence and respect?

Suggested textual analysis
Pages 129–131: beginning, "But Rubin Bailey's first teachings," and ending, "Surely it is all a question of know-how."

Why, after years of Rubin's teaching, does Allan lack confidence that he can be a sorcerer?

1. Why is it so difficult for Allan to accept that magic power is never guaranteed?

2. Why does Allan think his "native talent, which did not come from knowledge" is unreliable, even though Rubin praises this personal flair? (133)

3. Why are we told that Allan's experience of mistrusting his powers and fearing for his future often happens to apprentices? (133–134)

4. Why does Allan leave Rubin's house with a vision of failing Rubin, dishonoring his father, and being ridiculed by everyone else? Why, despite Rubin's teachings to the contrary, does Allan feel that "If a conjurer cannot conjure at will, he is worthless"? (134)

5. After he fails to cure Lizzie's baby, why does Allan tell his father that the magic has "never worked"? (139)

6. Why does Allan kiss his father after his failure to cure Lizzie's baby? Why does Allan feel guilty for arousing his father's emotions with this gesture? (139)

7. As he watches his father weep, why does Allan think, "Don't want me. . . . Don't love me as I am"? (141)

8. Why does the decision to live for the sake of his father lead Allan to experience the first spring of resignation, "the one thing the Sorcerer could not teach"? (142)

Suggested textual analysis
Pages 133–135: beginning, "The years passed," and ending, "You'll do fine."

Why does Allan resist the demons and choose not to destroy himself?

1. Why does Allan feel that if he cannot succeed as a magician, he must die?

2. Why does Allan think that being born in Africa or having been a slave might be necessary for becoming a sorcerer? (135)

3. On his way to conjuring up the demon kings, why does Allan think about how indebted he was to his father and how "he owed the universe far more than it owed him"? Why is Allan convinced that "To give was right; to ask wrong"? (140)

4. While conjuring up the demons, why does Allan think that his father is the "one he had truly harmed"? (140)

5. Why does the demon of the West suggest that "to love the good, the beautiful is right," but that Allan is "*beneath* this service" and is creating a monstrosity? (141)

6. Why does Allan's encounter with the demons bring him closer to his father?

7. Why are we told that Allan's attempt to comfort his father causes Richard to twitch back "in an old slave reflex"? (142)

8. Does Allan become a sorcerer?

Suggested textual analysis
Pages 140–142: from "Next he invoked the demon king of the North," to the end of the story.

FOR FURTHER REFLECTION

1. How does living with resignation promote the good?

2. What parallels white magic and sorcery in our lives: art? medicine? academia? social service? religious faith?

3. Do you have to resolve your relationship with your parents before you can be a success?

4. Does one become less obsessed with doing good as one grows older?

STAVROGIN'S CONFESSION

Fyodor Dostoevsky

FYODOR DOSTOEVSKY (1821–1881) was educated as a military engineer, but took little interest in engineering or the military. Instead, he wrote his first novel, *Poor Folk* (1846), which made him famous overnight and introduced the thematic and stylistic innovations that would ensure his lasting celebration. Dostoevsky was deeply troubled in his personal life. Condemned to death for his socialist beliefs, he was reprieved at the last moment but sentenced to four years in a Siberian prison. Subsequently, he experienced the deaths of his wife and brother, struggled with creditors, and had a serious gambling addiction. Out of this personal turmoil, he wrote a series of novels that carried literary art to new levels of psychological realism and complexity. Although he died well before the end of the nineteenth century, Dostoevsky's work reflects a profoundly modern consciousness, and he has been read as a precursor of psychoanalysis and existentialism. "Stavrogin's Confession" was originally meant to be a chapter of the novel *The Possessed* (also known as *The Devils*), but the editor of the journal in which the novel was being serialized refused to publish it. It was first published separately in 1922 after it was discovered among the papers left by Dostoevsky's wife.

Novel The Possessed

S

1

TAVROGIN[1] DID NOT SLEEP all that night. He sat on the sofa, his eyes fixed on one point in the corner by the chest of drawers. All night long the lamp burnt in his room. At about seven o'clock in the morning he fell asleep where he sat and when his valet Alexey Yegorovich, according to the once and for all established routine, entered his room at exactly half past nine with his morning cup of coffee, he opened his eyes and seemed unpleasantly surprised that he should have been asleep so long and that it was so late. He hastily drank his coffee, hastily dressed himself, and hurriedly left the house. To his valet's timid question, "Any orders, sir?" he made no reply. He walked along the street, his eyes fixed on the ground, deep in thought, and only when he occasionally raised his head did he suddenly show a certain vague but intense anxiety. At one crossing not far from his house a crowd of peasants, about fifty or more, crossed the

---

1. [Stavrogin, the central character of the novel *The Possessed*, is the charismatic but dissipated son of a wealthy society widow.]

road; they walked sedately, almost in silence, with calm deliberation. At a little shop, where he had to wait a moment, he heard someone say that they were "Shpigulin's workmen." He hardly paid any attention to them. At last, at about half past ten, he reached the gates of our St. Yefimyev Monastery of Our Lady, on the outskirts of the town, by the river. It was only there that he seemed to remember something that troubled and worried him. He stopped, hastily felt something in his side pocket, and— smiled. On entering the enclosure, he asked the first novice who happened to cross his path where he could find Bishop Tikhon, who was living in retirement in the monastery. The novice began bowing and immediately took him to see the bishop. Near the front steps at the end of the long two-storied monastery building a fat, gray-haired monk took him over authoritatively and promptly from the novice and led him along a long, narrow corridor, also bowing all the time, although because of his corpulence he could not bend low, but merely jerked his head frequently and abruptly. He went on begging him to follow, though Stavrogin was following him anyhow. The monk kept asking all sorts of questions and speaking of the Father Archimandrite, but, receiving no answer, became more and more deferential. Stavrogin could not help noticing that he was known here, although so far as he could remember he had only been there as a child. When they reached the door at the very end of the corridor, the monk opened it as though he were fully authorized to do so, inquired familiarly of the monk who looked after the bishop's rooms and who had rushed up to him whether they could go in, and without bothering to wait for a reply, flung the door wide open and, bending down, let the "dear" visitor pass. On receiving a gratuity, he quickly disappeared, as though in flight. Stavrogin entered a small room and almost at that very moment a tall, lean man appeared at the door of the adjoining room. He was about fifty-five, was wearing a simple indoor cassock, and looked a little ill. He smiled rather vaguely and had a strange, somewhat shy expression. This was Tikhon himself, the same Tikhon of whom Stavrogin had heard for the first time from Shatov and about whom he had since managed to pick up certain bits of information.

The information he had picked up was contradictory and of a rather varied nature, but it also seemed to have something in common, to wit, that those who liked and those who disliked Tikhon (and there were quite a few of those) were somehow not too keen to talk about him, those who disliked him probably because they did not think much of him, and those who were his supporters and even admirers out of a kind of considerateness, as though they were anxious to conceal something about him, some kind of weakness or even aberration. Stavrogin had found out that Tikhon had been living in the monastery for about six years and that the people who came to see him were ordinary peasants as well as persons of high social standing. Indeed, even in faraway Petersburg he had ardent admirers, though mostly among women. On the other hand, a portly elderly member of our club, a very pious one at that, expressed an opinion to the effect that "that Tikhon was practically insane and quite certainly fond of the bottle." Let me add here, although in anticipation, that the last statement was utter nonsense, but that the bishop did suffer from a chronic rheumatic affliction in the legs and was at times subject to some nervous spasms. Stavrogin also learnt that Tikhon had not been able to inspire any particular respect in the monastery itself either through weakness of character or "because of his absent-mindedness which was unforgivable and quite unnatural in a person of his rank."

It was said that the Father Archimandrite, a stern man who was very strict in regard to carrying out his duties as Father Superior and who was, besides, a well-known scholar, even seemed to feel a sort of hostility towards Tikhon and condemned him (not to his face, but indirectly) for his casual mode of life, and almost accused him of heresy. The attitude of the monks towards the saintly bishop was also, if not a little too casual, then at least, as it were, familiar. The two rooms which composed Tikhon's cell were also rather strangely furnished. Side by side with the heavy old bits of furniture, covered in worn leather, were three or four quite elegant pieces: a most expensive armchair, a large writing desk of excellent craftsmanship, an elegant carved bookcase, little tables, bookstands, all of which of course he had received as presents. There was a magnificent Bokhara carpet and next to it straw mats. There were engravings depicting scenes of "fashionable society" and mythological subjects, and near them, in the corner, a large icon case, glittering with silver and gold icons, one of which was of a very ancient date and contained relics. His library, too, it was said, was of too contradictory and diverse a character: next to the works of the great Christian saints and martyrs were "works of the stage and of fiction and, perhaps, even something much worse."

After the first greetings, exchanged for some reason with undisguised awkwardness on both sides, as well as hurriedly and even mumblingly, Tikhon led his visitor to his study and, still as it were in a hurry, made him sit on the sofa in front of the table, while sitting down himself nearby in a wicker armchair. At that moment Stavrogin, to his own surprise, got completely flustered. It looked as though he were trying with all his might to do something extraordinary and unavoidable and, at the same time, something that he found almost impossible to do. For a moment or two he looked round the study quite obviously unaware of anything he was looking at; he fell into thought, but perhaps he hardly knew what he was thinking about. It was the stillness in the room that roused him from his stupor and it seemed to him suddenly that Tikhon cast down his eyes shyly and with a smile that was quite out of place. This at once aroused in him a feeling of disgust and revolt; he felt like getting up and going away; in his view, Tikhon was quite decidedly drunk. But at that moment Tikhon raised his eyes and looked at him with a gaze so firm and full of thought and, at the same time, with so unexpected and enigmatic an expression, that he nearly gave a start. Then all of a sudden something quite different occurred to him: he felt that Tikhon already knew why he had come, that he had already been forewarned about it (though no one in the whole world could have known the reason) and, if he did not speak first, it was because he was sorry for him and fearful of his humiliation.

"Do you know who I am?" he suddenly asked abruptly. "Did I introduce myself when I came in or not? I'm sorry, I am so absent-minded . . ."

"You did not introduce yourself, but I had the pleasure of seeing you once four years ago, here in the monastery—by chance."

Tikhon spoke very slowly and evenly, in a soft voice, enunciating his words clearly and distinctly.

"I wasn't in this monastery four years ago," Stavrogin replied with what seemed like unnecessary discourtesy. "I was here only as a child long before you were here."

"Are you sure you haven't forgotten?" Tikhon asked guardedly and without insisting.

"No, I haven't forgotten," Stavrogin insisted for his part rather obstinately. "Why, it would be ridiculous not to remember. You must have just heard about me and formed some idea and that's why you imagined that you had seen me."

Tikhon said nothing. It was just then that Stavrogin noticed that Tikhon's face sometimes twitched nervously, a reminder of his breakdown some years before. "But I can see," he said, "that you are not well today. Perhaps it would be better if I went."

He was even about to get up from his chair.

"Yes, I had violent pains in my legs yesterday and today and I slept little during the night."

Tikhon stopped short. His visitor had suddenly sunk into a kind of strange reverie. The silence lasted for quite a long time, for two whole minutes.

"Why are you staring at me?" Stavrogin asked suddenly in alarm and suspiciously.

"I was looking at you and remembering what your mother looked like. You don't resemble one another, but there is a great deal of inner spiritual resemblance."

"No resemblance at all, certainly no spiritual—none whatever!" Stavrogin declared, looking worried and insisting again without reason and without knowing himself why. "You're just saying it out of—out of pity for my state of mind," he suddenly blurted out. "Good Lord, it must be my mother who visits you!"

"She does."

"I didn't know. She never said anything about it to me. Often?"

"Nearly every month. More often sometimes."

"She never, never told me. Never told me," he repeated, looking for some reason terribly alarmed by that fact. "I suppose you must have heard from her that I am insane," he blurted out again.

"No, not that you are insane. Still, I have heard that said, but by others."

"You must have an excellent memory if you can remember such trifles. Did you hear about that slap in the face too?"

"I did hear something about it."

"You've heard everything then. You must have had plenty of time to listen to all that. About the duel too?"

"About the duel too."

"You don't need newspapers here, do you? Did Shatov warn you about me?"

"No. I do know Mr. Shatov, though, but I haven't seen him for a long time."

"I see . . . What's that map you've got there? Ah, a map of the last war! What on earth do you want that for?"

"I was looking it up while reading this book. A most interesting description."

"Show me. Yes, not at all bad. A curious kind of reading for you, though."

He pulled the book towards him and cast a perfunctory glance at it. It was a lengthy and talented account of the circumstances of the last war, not so much from the military as from the literary point of view. After turning over a few pages, he suddenly threw the book down impatiently.

"I simply don't know what I've come here for," he said with an expression of disgust on his face, looking straight into Tikhon's eyes as though expecting an answer from him.

"You don't seem to be very well, either."

"Yes, I daresay."

And suddenly he told him, although rather briefly and abruptly, so that some of what he was saying was difficult to understand, that he was subject, especially at nights, to some kind of hallucinations, that he sometimes said or felt beside him the presence of some kind of malignant creature, mocking and "rational," "in all sorts of guises and in different characters, but it is the same, and it always makes me angry."

These revelations were wild and confused and really seemed to come from a madman. But at the same time Stavrogin spoke with such strange frankness, never seen in him before, with such simple-heartedness, which was so out of character as far as he was concerned, that one could not help feeling that his former self had suddenly and quite unaccountably completely disappeared. He was not at all ashamed of revealing the fear with which he talked about his apparition. But it was all a matter of a moment and it was gone as suddenly as it had come.

"It's all a lot of nonsense," he said quickly and with an awkward feeling of vexation, recollecting himself. "I must go and see a doctor."

"You certainly must," Tikhon agreed.

"You speak with such conviction. Have you met anyone like me with the same kind of apparitions?"

"I have, but very rarely. I remember only one man like that in my life. He was an army officer. I met him after he had lost his wife whom he badly missed. I've only heard of one other case like it. Both of them afterwards went abroad for medical treatment. How long have you suffered from this?"

"For about a year, but it's all a lot of nonsense. I shall go and see a doctor. It's all nonsense, utter nonsense. It's myself, different aspects of myself. Nothing more. You don't think, do you, that because I've just added that—er—phrase I'm still doubtful and not sure that it's me and not in fact the devil."

Tikhon looked up questioningly.

"Do you—do you really see him?" he asked in a tone of voice that implied that he did not doubt for a moment that it was nothing but an imagined, morbid hallucination. "Do you actually see some kind of image?"

"It's funny you should harp on it after I've already told you that I see it," Stavrogin said, growing more and more irritated with every word he uttered. "Of course I see it. I see it as plainly as I see you. Sometimes, though, I see it and yet I'm not sure that I see it, and sometimes I don't know which of us is real—me or him. It's all a lot of nonsense. Surely, you couldn't possibly have imagined that it really was the devil, could you?" he asked, laughing and passing a little too abruptly into a derisive tone of voice. "Well, I suppose it would be more in keeping with your profession, wouldn't it?"

"Most probably it is an illness, although . . ."

"Although what?"

"Devils most certainly exist, but one's idea of them may vary considerably."

"You lowered your eyes just now," Stavrogin interjected with an irritable laugh, "because you feel ashamed that while believing in the devil I should pretend not to believe in him and cunningly confront you with the question: does he or does he not really exist?"

Tikhon smiled vaguely.

"Well, I want you to know that I am not at all ashamed, and to make amends for my rudeness to you I'll tell you seriously and unashamedly: I do believe in the devil, I believe canonically, in a personal devil, not an allegory, and I have not the slightest desire to try to elicit an answer from anyone. That's all I want to make clear to you."

He gave an unnatural, nervous laugh. Tikhon looked at him with curiosity, but also, as it were, rather timidly and gently.

"Do you believe in God?" Stavrogin suddenly blurted out.

"I do."

"It is said, isn't it, that if you have faith and tell a mountain to move, it will move. . . . However, forgive me for all this nonsense. All the same I'm rather curious to know: will you or will you not move a mountain?"

"If God commands, I will," Tikhon said quietly and calmly, again dropping his eyes.

"Oh well, that's just the same as saying that God Himself will move it. No, no. What about you, you yourself? As a reward for your belief in God."

"Perhaps I won't move it."

"Perhaps? Well, that's not bad, either. However, you're still doubtful, aren't you?"

"I'm doubtful because of the imperfection of my belief."

"Good Lord, so you, too, don't believe absolutely?"

"Well, no. Perhaps I do not altogether believe absolutely," replied Tikhon.

"That I would never have suspected, looking at you," Stavrogin declared, glancing at him suddenly with some surprise, quite genuine surprise, which did not at all harmonize with the sarcastic tone of his preceding questions.

"Still, you at least believe that with God's assistance you will move, which is something. At any rate, you wish to believe. And you take the mountain literally too. It's an excellent principle. I have observed that the most advanced of our Levites show a strong inclination towards Lutheranism. All the same, this is better than the *très peu* of one of our archbishops, under the threat of the sword, it is true. I assume, of course, that you are also a Christian."

Stavrogin spoke rapidly, his words pouring out uninterruptedly, now seriously, now derisively.

"Of thy Cross, O Lord, may I not be ashamed," Tikhon almost whispered with a kind of passionate intensity, bowing his head still lower.

"But can one believe in the devil without believing in God?" Stavrogin said with a laugh.

"Oh, very much so," said Tikhon, raising his eyes and smiling. "You come across it everywhere."

"I'm sure you find such a belief more acceptable than complete disbelief," Stavrogin said, laughing loudly.

"On the contrary," Tikhon replied with unconcealed gaiety and good humor, "complete atheism is much more acceptable than worldly indifference."

"Oh, I see, so that's what you really think!"

"The absolute atheist stands on the last rung but one before most absolute faith (whether he steps higher or not), while an indifferent man has no faith at all, nothing but dismal fear, and that, too, only occasionally, if he is a sensitive man."

"I see . . . Have you read the Apocalypse?"

"I have."

"Do you remember: 'Write to the Angel of the Laodicean Church'?"

"I do."

"Where's the book?" Stavrogin asked, thrown into a strange hurry and anxiety and searching with his eyes for the book on the table. "I'd like to read you . . . You have a Russian translation, haven't you?"

"I know the passage, I remember it," said Tikhon.

"You know it by heart? Let me hear it."

He lowered his eyes quickly, rested both his hands on his knees, and impatiently prepared to listen. Tikhon recited it word for word.

"And unto the angel of the church of the Laodicean write: Those things saith the Amen, the faithful and true Witness, the beginning of the creation of God. I know thy works, that thou art neither cold nor hot: I would thou wert cold or hot. So that because thou art lukewarm, and neither cold nor hot, I will spue thee out of my mouth. Because thou sayest, I am rich and increased with goods, and have need of nothing; and knowest not that thou art wretched, and miserable and poor, and blind and naked . . ."

"Enough," Stavrogin cut him short. "I love you very much, you know."

"I love you too," Tikhon replied in a low voice.

Stavrogin fell silent and suddenly lapsed again into his old reverie. The same thing had happened fitfully before. This was the third time. He said "I love" to Tikhon as though in a trance. At least he never expected it himself. Over a minute passed.

"Don't be angry with me," whispered Tikhon, touching his elbow lightly with a finger and as though not really daring to do it.

Stavrogin started and frowned angrily.

"How did you know that I was angry?" he said quickly.

Tikhon was about to say something, but Stavrogin suddenly interrupted him in inexplicable alarm.

"Why did you assume that I simply had to be angry? Yes, I was furious. You are quite right. Just because I had said to you 'I love.' You are right, but you're a coarse cynic, you have a very low opinion of human nature. I might not have been furious, if I had not been myself but someone else. However, it is not a question of anyone else, but of me. All the same, you're an eccentric and quite crazy."

He was getting more and more irritated and, strangely, did not seem to care what he said.

"Listen, I don't like spies and psychologists, at least not those who creep into my soul. I don't invite anyone into my soul. I have no need of anyone. I can look after myself. You think I'm afraid of you," he went on, raising his voice and looking up defiantly. "You're quite convinced that I came to tell you some 'terrible secret,' and you are waiting for it with the monkish curiosity you are capable of. Well, then, I want you to know that I shall not reveal anything to you, no secret, for I can perfectly well do without you."

Tikhon looked at him firmly.

"You were surprised that the Lamb should love a cold man more than a merely lukewarm one," he said. "You don't want to be merely lukewarm. I can't help feeling that you are about to take an extreme, perhaps even a terrible, decision. I beg you not to torture yourself and to tell me everything."

"So you are quite sure that I have come with something."

"I . . . I guessed it," said Tikhon, lowering his eyes.

Stavrogin was rather pale, his hands trembled a little. For a few seconds he stared fixedly and in silence, as though on the point of taking a final decision. At last he took some printed sheets out of his side pocket and put them on the table.

"These are the sheets which are meant to be distributed," he said in a faltering voice. "I want you to know that if one man reads them I shall not conceal them any longer and they will be read by everyone. That's settled. I don't need you at all because my mind is made up. But do read them. Don't say anything while you're reading them. Tell me everything after you've read them."

"Shall I read?" Tikhon asked hesitantly.

"Yes, read. I don't mind."

"I'm afraid I shall not be able to read without my glasses. The print is very small. Foreign."

"Here are your glasses," Stavrogin said, handing him the glasses from the table and leaning against the back of the sofa. Tikhon did not look at him and became absorbed in the reading.

2

The print really was foreign: three sheets of ordinary notepaper printed and stitched together. It must have been printed secretly on some foreign press abroad. At the first glance the sheets of paper looked like some political pamphlet. [. . .] This is what Tikhon read:

From Stavrogin.

I, Nikolai Stavrogin, a retired army officer, lived in Petersburg in 186–, leading a life of dissipation in which I found no pleasure. At that time I had three lodgings during a certain period.

In one of them I lived myself, in furnished rooms with board and service. Maria Lebyatkin, my lawful wife, also lived there at the time. My other two lodgings I rented by the month to accommodate my two mistresses: in one I received a high society woman who was in love with me and in the other her maid, and for some time I toyed with the idea of bringing the two of them together, so that the society woman and her servant girl should meet each other in my rooms. Knowing the character of both, I anticipated a great deal of fun from that amusing encounter.

While secretly making all the necessary arrangements for that meeting, I had to visit more often one of the two lodgings in a large house in Gorokhovaya Street, for that was the place where I and the maid used to meet. I had only one room there on the fourth floor, which I rented from some Russian working-class people. They themselves lived in the next room, which was much smaller, so much so that the door dividing the two rooms was always open, which was what I wanted. The husband, who was working at some office, was away from morning till night. His wife, a woman of about forty, used to cut up old clothes and refashion them into new, and she used to leave the house quite often to deliver her sewing. I remained alone with her daughter, quite a child in appearance. Her name was Matryosha. Her mother loved her, but often chastised her and, as is customary with these people, shouted at her a lot. This little girl waited on me and made up my bed behind the screen. I declare that I have forgotten the number of the house. Having made some inquiries recently, I now know that the old house was pulled down and a new and very large house built on the site of two or three houses. I have also forgotten the name of my landlord (I may never have known it even at the time). I remember that the woman was called Stepanida and I believe her patronymic was Mikhailovna. I do not remember him. I suppose if one were seriously to make some inquiries at the Petersburg police stations, one might be able to trace them. Their flat was in the courtyard, in the corner. It all happened in June. The house was painted a light blue color.

One day I missed my penknife from the table. I did not want it at all. It was just lying about there. I told my landlady about it without thinking that she would thrash her daughter for it. But she had been screaming at her daughter for the loss of some rag and had even pulled her hair. But when that rag was found under the tablecloth, the little girl did not utter a word of complaint but just looked on in silence. I noticed that and it was then that I saw for the first time the little girl's face, which until that moment I had not particularly noticed. She had flaxen hair and a freckled face, quite an ordinary face, but it had a great deal of childishness in it, and it was very gentle, quite extraordinarily gentle. Her mother resented the fact that her daughter did not complain for having been beaten for nothing and she made as if to strike her with her fist, but stopped herself in time. It was just then that the subject of my penknife came up. There was no one in the flat besides the three of us. The little girl was the only one to go behind the screen in my room. The woman flew into a rage for having the first time punished the girl unjustly, rushed up to the besom, pulled some twigs out of it, and gave the girl a thrashing in front of me until her body was covered in weals, and that in spite of the fact that the girl was already in her twelfth year. Matryosha did not scream while she was being flogged, probably because I was there, but she gave a funny sort of sob at each blow. Afterwards she sobbed bitterly for a whole hour.

But before that happened something else caught my eye: at the very moment my landlady was rushing up to the besom to pull out the twigs, I saw my penknife on my bed where it must have fallen from the table. It occurred to me at once not to tell them about it so that she should be thrashed. I made my decision instantly; at such moments I always begin to breathe heavily. But I am determined to tell everything without flinching so that nothing should remain concealed any longer.

Every extraordinarily disgraceful, infinitely humiliating, vile, and, above all, ridiculous situation in which I happened to find myself in my life invariably aroused in me not only intense anger, but also a feeling of intense pleasure. It was the same in moments when I was committing a crime and in moments when my life was in danger. If I were to steal something, I should at the time of committing the theft have felt like dancing with pleasure at the thought of the depth of my villainy. It was not the villainy that I loved (here my mind was absolutely clear). What I liked was the feeling of rapture caused by the agonizing consciousness of my baseness. I felt just the same when, standing at the barrier, I waited for my opponent to fire: I experienced the same shameful and frenzied feeling, and on one occasion I did so with quite extraordinary force. I admit that I often sought it myself, for to me it was the strongest of any sensation of that kind. Whenever I received a slap in the face (and I received two in my life), it was there, too, in spite of my terrible anger. But I controlled my anger at the time, my feeling of pleasure exceeding anything that could be imagined. I never spoke to anyone about it, not even hinted at it, concealing it as something shameful and disgraceful. I did not experience that sensation but merely intense anger when I was once beaten up in a pub in Petersburg and dragged by the hair. Not being drunk, I merely put up a fight. But if I had been seized by the hair and forced down by the French vicomte who, when I was abroad, slapped me on the cheek and whose lower jaw I shot off for it, I should have experienced the same feeling of ecstasy and most likely have felt no anger at all. So it seemed to me then.

I am saying all this so that everyone should know that that feeling never got hold of me entirely, but that I always remained in control of my mental faculties (indeed, everything depends on that). Although it would take possession of me to a point of madness, to a point when it became an obsession, it would never be to a point when I lost control of myself entirely. When I was about to explode, I was able to overcome it entirely before it reached its climax. But I never wanted to stop it myself. I'm convinced that I could have lived all my life like a monk in spite of the brutish voluptuousness with which I have been endowed and which I always evoked. I am always master of myself when I want to be. And so I should like it to be known that I do not want to plead irresponsibility for my crimes either on the ground of my background or on the ground of illness.

The thrashing over, I put the penknife in my waistcoat pocket and, without uttering a word, left the house and threw it away in the street, having first walked a long way so that no one should ever find out. Then I waited two days. Having had a good cry, the little girl became even more taciturn; but I am sure she felt no resentment against me. I cannot help feeling, though, that she must have felt somewhat ashamed to have been punished in such a way in front of me. But I am sure that she blamed only herself for feeling ashamed, as any child would.

It was during those two days that I put to myself the question whether I should not go away and give up the plan I had devised. I felt immediately that I could, that I could give it up any time and at any moment. About that time I contemplated killing myself, for I was suffering from the disease of indifference, though I am not sure that that was the real reason. But during those two or three days (for I had to wait till the little girl had forgotten all about it) I committed a theft probably as a diversion from my obsession or maybe just for the fun of it. That was the only theft in my life.

A large number of people lived in those rooms. Among them was a civil servant with his family, who lived in two furnished rooms. He was about forty, not altogether a fool, of decent appearance, but poor. I did not become friends with him and he was afraid of the company that surrounded me there. He had only just drawn his salary of thirty-five rubles. What chiefly made me think of it was that at that particular moment I really needed money (though four days later I received money by post), so that I seemingly stole out of want and not for fun. It was done impudently and without any attempt at concealment. I simply entered his flat when he and his wife and children were having their dinner in the other little room. His folded uniform lay on a chair near the door. The idea occurred to me suddenly when I was still in the corridor. I put my hand into the pocket of his uniform and took out the purse. But the civil servant must have heard a slight movement, for he looked out of his room. I believe he did see at least something, but as he did not see it all, he did not, of course, believe his eyes. I said that I was passing down the corridor and had come to see the time by his clock. "I'm afraid it has stopped," he said. I went out.

I was drinking a great deal at the time and I always had a crowd of people in my rooms, Lebyatkin among them. I threw away the purse with the small change and kept the notes. There were thirty-two rubles, three red notes and two yellow. I changed a red note at once and sent out for champagne; then I sent the second red note and the third. Four hours later, in the evening, the civil servant was waiting for me in the corridor.

"You did not accidentally throw my uniform from the chair when you came in a few hours ago?" he asked. "I found it lying on the floor."

"I'm sorry I don't remember. Was your uniform there?"

"Yes, sir, it was."

"On the floor?"

"First on the chair, then on the floor."

"Did you pick it up?"

"I did."

"Well, so what more do you want?"

"Well, sir, in that case it's all right."

He dared not speak out and he dared not say anything to anybody in the house, so timid are these people. Anyhow, they were all terribly afraid of me in that house and respected me. Later I enjoyed exchanging glances with him in the corridor once or twice. Soon I got bored with it.

Three days later I returned to Gorokhovaya Street. The mother was going out somewhere with a bundle; her husband, of course, was not at home. Matryosha and I were alone in the flat. The windows were open. The house was full of workmen and all day long the sound of hammers and singing could be heard from all the floors. We had already been there for an hour. Matryosha sat in her small room on a little bench with her back to me and was busy with her needle. At last she suddenly began to sing softly, as she often did. I took out my watch and saw that it was two o'clock. My heart began to pound. I got up and began stealing towards her. On their windowsill were many pots of geraniums and the sun was shining very brightly. I sat down quietly on the floor beside her. She gave a start and at first looked terribly frightened and jumped up. I took her hand and kissed it quietly, forced her down on the bench again, and began looking into her eyes. The fact that I kissed her hand suddenly amused her like a child, but only for one second, for she jumped up precipitately the next moment, this time looking so frightened that a spasm passed across her face. Her eyes were motionless with terror and her lips began to quiver as though she were on the verge of tears, but she did not scream all the same. I kissed her hand again and put her on my knee. Then she suddenly drew back and smiled as if ashamed, but with a kind of wry smile. Her face flushed with shame. I was whispering to her all the time, as though drunk. At last a most strange thing happened, something I shall never forget, something that quite amazed me: the little girl flung her arms round my neck and all of a sudden began to kiss me frenziedly. Her face expressed complete rapture. I nearly got up and went away, so shocked was I to find this sort of thing in a little creature for whom I suddenly felt pity.

When all was over, she looked embarrassed. I did not try to reassure her and no longer caressed her. She looked at me, smiling timidly. Her face suddenly appeared stupid to me. She was getting more and more embarrassed with every minute that passed. At last she covered her face with her hands and stood motionless in a corner with her face to the wall. I was afraid she might be frightened again as she had been a short while earlier, and silently left the house.

I can only imagine that all that had happened to her must have seemed utterly hideous, a deathlike horror. In spite of the Russian swearwords which she must have heard from her very cradle and all sorts of strange conversations, I am quite convinced that she did not yet understand anything. I am sure that in the end it must have seemed to her that she had committed a terrible crime and was guilty of a mortal sin. "She had killed God."

That night I had that punch up in the pub which I have mentioned in passing. But I woke up in my rooms in the morning: Lebyatkin had taken me home. On awakening my first thought was: had she told them or not? It was a moment of real fear, though as yet not very intense. I was very gay that morning and terribly kind to everybody, and the whole gang was very pleased with me. But I left them all and went to Gorokhovaya Street. I met her downstairs in the entrance hall. She was coming from the shop where she had been sent for chicory. On catching sight of me, she looked terribly frightened and ran off upstairs. When I entered, her mother had already bashed her for rushing in like mad, which helped to conceal the real reason for her fright. So far then everything was all right. She seemed to have hidden herself away somewhere and did not come in while I was there. I stayed there for an hour and then went away.

Towards evening I was again overcome by fear, this time incomparably more intense. No doubt I could have denied it all, but I might be found out and I could already see myself as a convict in a Siberian prison. I had never felt fear and, except for this incident in my life, I never before or after was afraid of anything. Certainly not of Siberia, though I might have been sent there more than once. But this time I was frightened and really felt fear, I don't know why, for the first time in my life—a very painful feeling. Besides, I conceived such a hatred for her that evening in my room that I decided to kill her. The recollection of her smile was the chief reason for my hatred. I began to feel contempt and intense loathing for her because after it was all over she had rushed off to a corner of the room and covered her face with her hands. I was seized with an inexplicable rage, then I became feverish, and when towards morning I began to feel that I had a temperature, I was again overcome by panic which became so intense that I never experienced a torment more violent. But I no longer hated the little girl, at least my hatred did not reach such a paroxysm as on the previous evening. I perceived that intense fear completely ousts hatred and the feeling of revenge.

I woke about midday feeling well and was surprised at the force of yesterday's sensations. However, I was in a bad mood and again felt compelled to go to Gorokhovaya Street in spite of all my aversion. I remember that I wanted terribly to have a quarrel with someone on the way, a real violent quarrel. But on arriving at Gorokhovaya Street I unexpectedly found there Nina Savelyevna, the maid, who had been waiting for me for an hour. I did not love that girl at all and she was afraid that I might be angry with her for coming unasked. But I suddenly felt very glad to see her. She was not bad-looking, modest and with the manners the lower middle classes set such store by, so that my landlady had been telling me for a long time what a nice girl she was. I found them both having coffee together and my landlady highly pleased with their pleasant conversation. In the corner of their small room I caught sight of Matryosha. She stood gazing motionless at her mother and the visitor. When I came in she did not hide herself as before and did not run away. I could not help observing that she had grown very thin and that she had a temperature. I was nice to Nina and locked the door leading into the landlady's room, which I had not done for a long time, so that Nina left looking very happy. I saw her off myself and did not return to Gorokhovaya Street for two days. I was bored with the whole business. I decided to put an end to it all by giving up my rooms and leaving Petersburg.

But when I came to give notice I found my landlady greatly worried and upset. Matryosha had been ill for three days; she had a high temperature and was delirious at night. I asked of course what she said in her delirium (we were talking in whispers in my room), and she whispered that her daughter was saying "terrible things," such as "I killed God." I offered to call a doctor at my own expense, but she would not hear of it. "God willing, it will pass, she isn't in bed all the time, she goes out during the day, she has just run round to the shop." I made up my mind to see Matryosha alone and, as the landlady informed me in passing that she had to go to a Petersburg suburb about five o'clock, I decided to come back in the evening.

I had lunch in a pub. Exactly at a quarter past five I returned. I always let myself in with my key. There was no one there except Matryosha. She was lying in the small room on her mother's bed behind the screen and I saw her looking out. But I pretended not to have noticed. All the windows were open. The air was warm, even hot. I paced the room for a while and then sat down on the sofa. I remember everything to the last moment. It positively gave me pleasure not to talk to Matryosha but to keep her in suspense. I don't know why. I waited for a whole hour when she suddenly rushed out from behind the screen herself. I heard both her feet hit the floor when she jumped out of bed, then her fairly quick steps, and presently she stood on the threshold of my room. She stood and gazed in silence. I was so mean that my heart missed a beat with joy: I was so glad that I had not given in and waited for her to come out first. During the days that I had not seen her even once so close since our last meeting, she really had grown very thin. Her face had shrunk and her head, I was quite certain, was hot.

Her eyes had grown large and she gazed at me without blinking with a dull curiosity, as I thought at first. I sat still, looked, and did not move. Then suddenly I again felt that I hated her. But very soon I realized that she was not a bit afraid of me, though she was perhaps still delirious. But she was not delirious at all. She suddenly began shaking her head at me, as ingenuous and unmannered people do when they disapprove of someone. Then suddenly she raised her tiny fist and began shaking it at me from where she stood. At first this gesture seemed ridiculous to me, but soon I could stand it no longer. Her face was full of such despair which was quite unbearable to see on the face of a child. She was still shaking her fist at me threateningly and shaking her head reproachfully. I got up, took a few steps towards her in fear, and began speaking cautiously to her, quietly and kindly, but I realized that she wouldn't understand. Then suddenly she covered her face impulsively with both hands as she had done at that time, moved off, and stood at the window with her back to me. I went back to my room and also sat down at the window. I simply cannot understand why I did not leave then, but remained as though waiting for something. Soon I again heard her quick steps. She went out through the door onto the wooden landing at the top of the stairs. I ran up to my door at once, opened it a little, and was just in time to see Matryosha go into the tiny box-room, which was like a hencoop, next to the lavatory. A very curious thought flashed through my mind. To this day I cannot understand why it should have come into my head so suddenly. So it would seem that it was at the back of my mind all the time. I left the door ajar and again sat down by the window. Of course it was still impossible to believe in the thought that had flashed through my mind, "but still . . ." (I remember everything, and my heart beat violently).

A minute later I looked at my watch and made a note of the time with absolute accuracy. Why I had to know the time so exactly I can't tell, but I seem to have been able to do so and, anyway, at that moment I wanted to make a note of everything. So that I remember now what I observed and I can see it as if it were happening at this moment. The evening was drawing in. A fly was buzzing over my head and kept settling on my face. I caught it, held it in my fingers, and put it out of the window. Very loudly a cart drove into the yard. Very loudly (and for some time before) a tailor, sitting at a window in the corner of the yard, sang a song. He sat at his work and I could see him. It occurred to me that since no one had seen me when I walked through the gates and went upstairs, it was quite unnecessary for anyone to see me when I should be going downstairs. I moved my chair quietly from the window so that I could not be seen by the lodgers. I picked up a book, but put it down again and began looking at a tiny red spider on the leaf of a geranium and lost count of the time. I remember everything to the very last moment.

Suddenly I whipped out my watch. Twenty minutes had passed since she went out of the room. My guess was assuming the aspect of reality. But I decided to wait for exactly another quarter of an hour. It had also crossed my mind that she might have returned and that I might have failed to hear her. But that was impossible: there was dead silence and I could hear the whir of every midge. Suddenly my heart started pounding again. I took out my watch: there were three minutes to go. I sat them out, though my heart was pounding painfully. Then I got up, put on my hat, buttoned my overcoat, and looked round the room to make sure that I had left no trace of my presence there. I moved the chair nearer to the window just as it had stood there before. At last I opened the door quietly, locked it with my key, and went up to the little box-room. It was closed, but not bolted. I knew that it was never bolted, but I did not want to open it. I stood on tiptoe and began looking through the chink. At that very moment, just as I raised myself on my toes, I recalled that when I sat at the window and looked at the little red spider and then lost count of the time, I had been thinking how I should stand on tiptoe and look through this chink. In putting in this trifling detail I want to prove without a shadow of doubt to what an extent I was quite clearly in the full possession of my mental faculties and how much I am responsible for everything. I looked through the chink a long time, for it was very dark there, but not so dark as to prevent me at last from seeing what I wanted. . . .

At last I decided to leave. I came across no one on the stairs. Three hours later we were all drinking tea in our shirtsleeves in our rooms and playing with a pack of old cards. Lebyatkin recited poems. We were telling lots of stories, all of them, as it happened, clever and amusing and not as foolish as usual. No one was drunk, though there was a bottle of rum on the table, Lebyatkin alone helping himself to it.

Prokhor Malov once observed that "when Stavrogin is contented and not depressed, all our lads are cheerful and talk cleverly." I remembered it at that time which shows that I was cheerful and contented and not depressed. This was what it looked like from the outside. But I remember that I was conscious of being a low and despicable coward simply because I was glad of having escaped and that I should never again be an honorable man (neither here, nor after death, nor ever). And something else happened to me at the time: it seems that the Jewish saying, "The thing you do may be bad, but it doesn't smell," just fitted me. For although I felt that I was a scoundrel, I was not ashamed of it and not in the least upset. When sitting at the tea table and chattering away with them, I formulated for the first time in my life what appeared to be the rule of my life, namely, that I neither know nor feel good or evil and that I have not only lost any sense of it, but that there is neither good nor evil (which pleased me), and that it is just a prejudice: that I can be free from any prejudice, but that once I attain that degree of freedom I am done for. This I formulated for the first time at that very moment when we were all having tea, when I laughed so much and talked such a lot of nonsense with them. But that is also why I remember it all. Old ideas which everyone knows often suddenly appear as if they were quite new, sometimes even after one has lived for fifty years.

But all the time I was waiting for something. So it came about that at eleven o'clock the houseporter's little daughter came running from my landlady in Gorokhovaya Street with the news that Matryosha had hanged herself. I went with the little girl and saw that the landlady herself did not know why she had sent for me. She wailed and screamed hysterically; there were lots of people and policemen. I remained there for a while and then went away.

The police scarcely troubled me, though I had to answer the usual questions. But except that the girl was ill and at times delirious and that I had offered to call a doctor at my expense, I said nothing that might have been taken down in evidence.

They did question me about myself and the penknife. I told them that my landlady had given the girl a beating, but that that was nothing. No one knew of my having been there that evening.

For about a week I did not call round there. I went there long after the funeral to give notice. The landlady was still crying, although she was already busying herself as usual with her rags and her sewing. "You see, sir," she said to me, "I hurt her feelings because of your penknife." But she did not seem to blame me particularly. I settled my account and gave as my excuse for leaving that I could not possibly receive Nina Savelyevna after what had happened in the house. She said again a few nice things about Nina Savelyevna at parting. Before leaving, I gave her five rubles over and above what I owed her.

The main thing was that I was bored with life, sick and tired to death of it. I should have completely forgotten the incident in Gorokhovaya Street after the danger had passed just as I had forgotten everything else that happened at the time, if I had not kept remembering angrily what a coward I had been.

I vented my anger on anyone I could. It was at that time, but not for any particular reason, that I took it into my head to ruin my life somehow or other, but only in as disgusting a way as possible. A year earlier I had been thinking of shooting myself; however, something better turned up.

One day, looking at Maria Lebyatkin, who occasionally did some charring in my rooms and who in those days had not yet gone mad but was just an ecstatic idiot who was madly in love with me in secret (which my friends had found out), I suddenly decided to marry her. The idea of the marriage of Stavrogin to a low creature like that excited my nerves. One could not imagine anything more outrageous. At all events I did not marry her merely because of "a bet for a bottle of wine after a drunken dinner." Kirilov and Peter Verkhovensky, who happened to be in Petersburg at the time, as well as Lebyatkin and Prokhor Malov (now dead) acted as witnesses. No one else ever knew anything about it, and they gave me their word to say nothing about it. The silence always seemed to me rather disgusting, but it has not been broken till now, though I did intend to make it public. I do so now together with the rest.

After the wedding I left for the country to stay with my mother. I left because I wanted some distraction. In our town I left behind me the idea that I was mad, an idea that still persists and that undoubtedly does me harm, as I shall explain later. Then I went abroad and spent four years there.

I went to the East, to Mount Athos, where I stood through midnight masses which went on for eight hours. I went to Egypt, lived in Switzerland, went even to Iceland; I spent a whole year in Goettingen University. During the last year I struck up an acquaintance with an aristocratic Russian family in Paris and two young Russian girls in Switzerland. About two years ago, passing a stationer's shop in Frankfurt, I noticed among the photographs for sale a portrait of a little girl, wearing an elegant dress but looking very like Matryosha. I bought the photograph at once and, on returning to my hotel room, I placed it on the mantelpiece. There it lay untouched for a whole week. I never once looked at it and when I left Frankfurt I forgot to take it with me.

I mention it only to show to what an extent I could get the better of my memories and how indifferent I had become to them. I repudiated them all en masse and the whole pile of them obediently disappeared every time I wanted it to disappear. I always found my memories of the past boring and I never could discuss the past as almost everybody does, particularly as it was so hateful to me, like everything else that concerned me. As for Matryosha, I even forgot her photograph on the mantelpiece. One spring, traveling through Germany a year ago, I absent-mindedly went on past the station where I had to change trains and found myself on the wrong line. I got out at the next station. It was past two o'clock in the afternoon, a bright, lovely day. It was a tiny German town. I was shown to a hotel. I had to wait, for the next train was not due before eleven o'clock at night. I was quite glad of my adventure, for I was not in any particular hurry to go anywhere. The hotel was very small and rather shabby, but it was all covered in greenery and surrounded with flower beds. I was given a very small room. I had an excellent meal and as I had been traveling all night I soon fell sound asleep at four o'clock in the afternoon.

I had quite an extraordinary dream. I had never had one like it before. In the Dresden gallery there is a picture by Claude Lorraine, called, I think, *Acis and Galatea*[2] in the catalogue. I always called it The Golden Age. I don't know why. I had seen it before, but now, three days before, as I passed through Dresden, I saw it again. I went specially to the gallery to have a look at it and for all I know I must have stopped at Dresden for the sole purpose of seeing it again. It was that picture that I saw in my dream, not as a painting, but as a fact.

A corner of the Greek archipelago—blue, caressing waves, island and rocks, a foreshore covered in lush vegetation, a magic vista in the distance, a spellbinding sunset—it is impossible to describe it in words. Here was the cradle of European civilization, here were the first scenes from mythology, man's paradise on earth. Here a beautiful race of men had lived. They rose and went to sleep happy and innocent; the woods were filled with their joyous songs, the great overflow of their untapped energies passed into love and unsophisticated gaiety. The sun shed its rays on these islands and that sea, rejoicing in its beautiful children. A wonderful dream, a sublime illusion! The most incredible dream that has ever been dreamed, but to which all mankind has devoted all its powers during the whole of its existence, for which it has sacrificed everything, for which it has died on the cross, and for which its prophets have been killed, without which nations will not live and cannot even die. I seem to have lived through all these sensations in my dream; I do not know what exactly I dreamed about, but the rocks and the sea and the slanting rays of the setting sun—I still seemed to see them all

---

2. [Acis was a Sicilian youth beloved by the nymph Galatea and slain by Polyphemus, a Cyclops who was jealous of his success.]

when I woke and opened my eyes, which were literally wet with tears for the first time in my life. A sensation of happiness that I had never experienced before went right through my heart till it hurt. It was already evening; through the window of my little room, through the green leaves of the flowers on the windowsill, a whole bunch of bright slanting rays of the setting sun poured upon me and bathed me in light. I shut my eyes quickly once more as though panting to bring back the vanished dream, but suddenly in the center of that bright, bright light I beheld a tiny point. Suddenly the point began to take on a kind of shape, and all at once I could clearly see a tiny red spider. I immediately remembered the red spider on the leaf of the geranium which was also bathed in the rays of the setting sun. I felt as if something had gone right through me. I raised myself and sat on my bed. . . .

(That is all how it happened then!)

I saw before me (Oh, not really! Oh, if it had only been a real phantom!) Matryosha, emaciated and with feverish eyes, exactly as she was when she stood on the threshold of my room and, shaking her head, shook her tiny fist at me. Nothing has ever been so distressing to me! The pathetic despair of a helpless creature with an unformed mind threatening me (with what? what could she do to me, O Lord?), but blaming of course only herself! Nothing like that has ever happened to me. I sat there till nightfall without moving and forgetful of the time. I do not know and I cannot tell to this day whether this is what is called remorse or repentance. But what I find so unbearable is the image of her standing on the threshold and threatening me with her small raised fist, just the way she looked at me then, just that shaking of her head. It is this that I cannot stand, for since then it has appeared to me almost every day. It doesn't come itself. I myself summon it up and I cannot help summoning it up though I cannot live with it. Oh, if only I could ever see her real self, even if it were a hallucination!

Why then does not any memory of my life arouse in me anything like this? Have I not had many memories, some of them perhaps much worse in the judgment of men? Why only one hatred and that one, too, stirred up by my present state, for before I forgot it cold-bloodedly and dismissed it out of hand?

I wandered about after that for almost a whole year and tried to find some occupation. I know that I can dismiss Matryosha from my mind any time I wish. I am as much in command of my will as ever. But the whole point is that I never wanted to do so, I do not want to myself and never shall want to. It will go on like that till I lapse into madness.

Two months later in Switzerland I had an outburst of the same kind of passion accompanied by the same kind of uncontrollable impulses as I used to have in the past before. I felt a terrible temptation to commit a new crime, namely, to enter into a bigamous marriage (for I was already married); but I fled on the advice of another girl whom I told almost everything, even that I was not at all in love with the girl whom I desired so much and that I could never love anyone. Besides, that new crime would not have rid me of Matryosha.

I therefore decided to have these pages printed and take three hundred copies of them to Russia. When the time comes I shall send some of them to the police and the local authorities; simultaneously I shall send them to the editors of all the newspapers with a request to publish them, and to many persons in Petersburg and in Russia who know me. It will also be published abroad in translation. I realize that legally I have nothing to fear, not to any considerable extent at any rate. It is I alone who am informing against myself, for I have no accuser; besides, there is no evidence against me, or what there is is extremely slight. There is, finally, the prevailing idea that I am not in my right mind, an idea which I am quite sure my family will make use of in their efforts to quash any legal prosecution that might be dangerous to me. I make this statement, incidentally, in order to prove that I am in full possession of my mental faculties and realize my position. So far as I am concerned, there will remain those who will know everything and they will look at me and I at them. I want everyone to look at me.

Whether it will make things easier for me I do not know. I fall back on it as my last resource.

Once more: if a thorough search were made in the records of the Petersburg police something might perhaps be discovered. Matryosha's parents may still be living in Petersburg. The house, of course, will be remembered. It was painted a light blue color. As for me, I shall not go anywhere and for some time (for a year or two) I shall always be found at Skvoreshniki, my mother's estate. If summoned, I will appear anywhere.

NIKOLAI STAVROGIN

3

The reading went on for about an hour. Tikhon read slowly and, perhaps, read some passages twice over. All that time Stavrogin sat silent and motionless. Strangely enough, the trace of impatience, absent-mindedness, and even delirium that had been on his face all the morning had almost disappeared, being replaced by calmness and a kind of sincerity that gave him an air almost of dignity. Tikhon took off his glasses and began to speak, at first rather guardedly.

"Don't you think certain corrections could be made in this document?"

"Why?" asked Stavrogin. "I wrote sincerely."

"In the style perhaps a little?"

"I forgot to warn you," Stavrogin said quickly and sharply with a forward thrust of his body, "that all you say will be useless. I shall not give up my intention. Don't try to dissuade me. I shall publish it."

"You did not forget to warn me about it before I began to read."

"Never mind," Stavrogin interrupted harshly. "Let me repeat again: however strong your objections may be, I shall not give up my intention. Please note that by this happy or unhappy phrase—think of it what you like—I am not at all trying to suggest you should start at once objecting or attempt to persuade me."

"I could hardly raise any objections or try to persuade you to give up your intentions. The idea of yours is a great idea, nor could a Christian idea be expressed more perfectly. Further than the wonderful act of heroism you have conceived repentance cannot go unless . . ."

"Unless what?"

"Unless it was in fact repentance and in fact a Christian idea."

"I wrote sincerely."

"You seem to wish to make yourself out to be worse than your heart would desire," said Tikhon, gradually growing bolder: the "document" had evidently made a strong impression on him.

"Make myself out to be? I repeat: I did not 'make myself out to be' and I certainly did not try to 'show off.' "

Tikhon quickly cast his eyes down.

"This document comes straight from a heart which has been mortally wounded—do I understand you right?" he said emphatically and with extraordinary warmth. "Yes, this is repentance and the natural need for it that has got the better of you, and you have taken the great road, a miraculous road. But you seem already to hate and despise beforehand all those who will read what you have described here and to challenge them to battle. You were not ashamed to confess your crime, why are you ashamed of repentance?"

"Ashamed?"

"Yes, ashamed and afraid."

"Afraid?"

"Terribly. Let them look at me, you say. But what about you? How will you look at them? Some passages in your statement are overstressed. You seem to be admiring your psychology and clutching at every detail merely with the intention of surprising your reader by a callousness which is not in you. What else is this but a proud challenge by an accused to the judge?"

"Where's the challenge? I eliminated all personal discussions."

Tikhon made no answer. His pale cheeks flushed.

"Let's drop it," Stavrogin dismissed it sharply. "Let me now ask you a question. We've been talking for five minutes since you read that," he nodded in the direction of the sheets of paper, "and I cannot detect any expression of shame or aversion in you. You're not very squeamish, are you?"

He did not finish.

"I shall conceal nothing from you: what horrified me was the vast unused energy that was deliberately spent on some abomination. As for the crime itself, many people sin like that, but they live in peace and quiet with their conscience, even considering it the unavoidable misdemeanors of youth. There are also old men who sin the same way, not taking it seriously and regarding it as innocent amusement. The whole world is full of these horrors. But you felt the whole depth of your degradation which is extremely rare."

"You haven't begun respecting me after what you've been reading, have you?" Stavrogin said with a wry smile.

"I'm not going to give you a straight answer to this. But there certainly is not, nor can there be, any greater or more terrible crime than what you did to that girl."

"Let's stop judging people by our own yardstick. Perhaps I do not suffer as much as I've written and perhaps I really have told a lot of lies about myself," he added unexpectedly.

Tikhon again made no comment.

"And what about the girl with whom you broke off in Switzerland?" Tikhon began again. "Where, may I ask, is she at this moment?"

"She's here."

Again there was silence.

"Perhaps I did tell you a lot of lies about myself," Stavrogin repeated insistently. "Still, what does it matter if I do challenge them by the coarseness of my confession, seeing that you have noticed the challenge? I shall make them hate me even more, that's all. That ought to make things easier for me."

"You mean spite in you will rouse spite in others and, hating them, you will feel happier than if you had accepted their pity."

"You're right. You know," he laughed suddenly, "they may perhaps call me a jesuit and a sanctimonious hypocrite after the document. Ha, ha, ha! Don't you think so?"

"Why, of course, there's sure to be such an opinion. And how soon do you hope to carry out your intention?"

"Today, tomorrow, the day after tomorrow, how do I know? Very soon, though. You're right. I think it will indeed happen like that: I shall make it public suddenly and indeed in some revengeful and hateful moment when I hate them most."

"Answer me one question, but sincerely, me alone, only me," Tikhon said in quite a different tone of voice. "If anyone forgave you for this," Tikhon pointed at the sheets of paper, "not anyone whom you respect or fear, but a complete stranger, someone you will never know, who, reading your terrible confession, forgave you inwardly, in silence, would that make you feel better or would it make no difference to you?"

"Better," replied Stavrogin in an undertone. "If you forgave me," he added, lowering his eyes, "I'd feel much better too."

"On condition that you forgave me also," Tikhon said in a voice full of emotion.

"False humility! These monastic formulas, you know, are not at all elegant. Let me tell you the whole truth: I want you to forgive me and one, two, or three others with you, but not everybody else—I'd rather everybody else hated me. I want this so that I should be able to bear it with humility. . . ."

"And what about universal pity for you? Would you not be able to bear that with the same kind of humility?"

"Perhaps I could not. But why do you . . ."

"I feel the extent of your sincerity and I am, of course, much to blame for not being able to approach people. I've always felt it to be a great fault in myself," Tikhon said with great sincerity, looking straight into Stavrogin's eyes. "I'm saying this only because I'm terribly afraid for you," he added. "There's almost an impassable abyss before you."

"You don't think I shall be able to stand it? That I shan't be able to bear their hatred?" Stavrogin said with a start.

"Not only hatred."

"What else?"

"Their laughter," Tikhon almost forced himself to say in a very soft whisper.

Stavrogin looked embarrassed; his face expressed alarm.

"I knew you'd say that," he said. "So you thought me a very comical person after reading my 'document,' did you? Don't worry and don't look so disconcerted. I expected it."

"The horror will be general and, needless to say, more false than sincere. People fear only what directly threatens their interests. I'm not talking of pure souls: they will be horrified inwardly and accuse themselves, but they will not be noticed, for they will be silent. But the laughter will be universal."

"I'm surprised what a low opinion you have of people, how loathsomely you regard them," Stavrogin said with some bitterness.

"I know you won't believe me," cried Tikhon, "but I judged more by myself than by other people."

"Did you? Is there also something deep inside you that makes you amused at my misfortune?"

"Who knows? Perhaps there is. Oh, perhaps there is!"

"Enough. Show me what it is exactly that strikes you as ridiculous in my manuscript. I know what it is myself, but I want you to put your finger on it. And say it as cynically as possible. Indeed, say it with all the sincerity of which you are capable. And let me tell you again that you are a terrible eccentric."

"Why, even in the form of this great penance there is something ridiculous. Oh, don't try to persuade yourself that you won't emerge victorious from it," he cried suddenly, almost beside himself. "Even this form," he pointed to the manuscript, "will triumph provided you sincerely accept the contumely and the vituperation. It always ended in the most ignominious cross becoming a great glory and a great force, if the humility of the great deed was sincere. It is quite possible that you will be comforted even in your lifetime."

"So you think there's something ridiculous perhaps in the form alone, do you?" Stavrogin insisted.

"And in the substance. The ugliness will kill it," Tikhon whispered, lowering his eyes.

"Ugliness? What ugliness?"

"Of the crimes. There are crimes that are truly ugly. Crimes, whatever their nature, are more impressive, more, as it were, picturesque, the more blood and the more horror. But there are crimes that are shameful and disgraceful quite apart from the horror, crimes that are, as it were, a little too inelegant. . . ."

Tikhon stopped short.

"You mean," Stavrogin broke in excitedly, "you find that I cut a rather ridiculous figure when I kissed the hand of a dirty little girl. I understand you very well. You despair of me just because it is so ugly, so loathsome. No, I don't mean that it is loathsome, but that it is shameful and ridiculous. You think it is this that I shall be able to bear least of all."

Tikhon was silent.

"Now I understand why you asked me about the girl from Switzerland. I mean, whether she was here."

"You're not prepared, not hardened," Tikhon whispered timidly. "You're uprooted, you do not believe."

"Listen, Father Tikhon: I want to forgive myself. That is my chief purpose, my only purpose!" Stavrogin said suddenly, with gloomy rapture in his eyes. "I know that only then will the apparition vanish. That is why I seek boundless suffering. Seek it myself. Don't try to frighten me or spite will kill me."

The sincerity of his outburst was so unexpected that Tikhon got up.

"If you believe," Tikhon exclaimed rapturously, "that you can forgive yourself and obtain that forgiveness for yourself in this world through suffering, if you set that purpose before you with faith, then you believe in everything already. Why, then, did you say that you did not believe in God?"

Stavrogin made no answer.

"God will forgive you for your unbelief, for you respect the Holy Spirit without knowing Him."

"By the way, Christ will forgive, won't He?" asked Stavrogin with a wry smile, quickly changing his tone, and there was an unmistakable touch of irony in the tone of his question.

"It says in the Book, 'And whosoever shall offend one of these little ones'—remember. According to the Gospel, there is no greater crime."

"You simply don't want a good old row and you're laying a trap for me, dear old Father Tikhon," Stavrogin mumbled casually and with annoyance, trying to get up. "In short, what you want is that I should settle down, get married, and end my days as a member of our club, visiting your monastery on every church festival. Real to goodness church penance! Isn't that so? Still, as an expert in the human heart you foresee, no doubt, that it will certainly be so and that all that remains to be done now is to ask me nicely, just as a matter of form, for I am only waiting to be asked, isn't that so?"

He chuckled affectedly.

"No, it isn't that kind of penance," Tikhon cried warmly, without taking any notice of Stavrogin's laugh and remark. "I'm getting quite another one ready for you. I know an elder, not here, but not far from here, a hermit and an ascetic, a man of such great Christian wisdom as is beyond your or my understanding. He will listen to my entreaties. I'll tell him everything about you. Go to him, share his retreat as a novice, stay under his guidance for five or seven years, for as long as you may find necessary yourself. Take a vow and by this great sacrifice you will acquire everything you crave for and even what you do not expect, for you cannot possibly conceive now what you will obtain."

Stavrogin heard him out gravely.

"You propose that I enter that monastery as a monk."

"You need not live in the monastery, you need not take your vows as a monk, you can be just a novice, a secret, not an open one. It can be arranged for you to go on living in society. . . ."

"Leave me alone, Father Tikhon," Stavrogin interrupted him, looking disgusted and getting up. Tikhon also got up.

"What's the matter with you?" Stavrogin suddenly cried, looking intently at Tikhon almost in fear.

Tikhon stood before him, his hands clasped in front of him, a painful spasm passing for a moment across his face as though from a terrible fright.

"What's the matter with you? What's the matter?" Stavrogin kept repeating, rushing forward to support him. He thought that Tikhon was going to fall.

"I see, I see, just as if it were happening in front of me now," Tikhon cried in a voice that penetrated the soul and with an expression of great sadness, "that you, poor, lost youth, have never been so near another and still greater crime as you are at this moment."

"Calm yourself," pleaded Stavrogin, who was really alarmed for him. "Perhaps I shall still postpone it . . . You're quite right. . . ."

"No, not after the publication, but before it. A day, an hour perhaps before the great step, you will commit a new crime as a way out, and you will commit it solely in order to avoid the publication of these pages."

Stavrogin was shaking with anger and almost with fear.

"You damned psychologist!" he cut him short suddenly in a rage and, without looking back, left the cell. ∽

INTERPRETIVE QUESTIONS
FOR DISCUSSION

Why does Stavrogin seduce Matryosha and then abandon her to despair?

1. Why does Stavrogin notice Matryosha for the first time when she does not utter a word of complaint despite the fact that her mother has beaten her unjustly? Why does he particularly notice that her face was childish and extraordinarily gentle? (164)

2. Why does Stavrogin hide the discovery of his penknife so that Matryosha will be beaten again? (164)

3. Why does "every extraordinarily disgraceful, infinitely humiliating, vile, and, above all, ridiculous situation" in which Stavrogin finds himself arouse in him not only intense anger, but also "a feeling of intense pleasure"? (164–165)

4. Why, before seducing Matryosha, does Stavrogin ask himself whether he should go away and give up the plan he has devised? Why, at about the same time, does he contemplate killing himself? (166)

5. Why is Stavrogin shocked when Matryosha responds to his blandishments by kissing him frenziedly and with complete rapture? (168)

6. Why does the recollection of her smile and her gesture of covering her face with her hands after their encounter cause Stavrogin to conceive such a hatred for Matryosha that he resolves to kill her? (169)

7. Why does Stavrogin return to Matryosha's apartment, but then pretend not to notice her? Why does it give him pleasure not to talk to her, "but to keep her in suspense"? (171)

8. Why does Stavrogin make a feeble attempt to reassure Matryosha "in fear," but then give up, thinking "she wouldn't understand"? (171–172)

9. Why is it impossible for Stavrogin to believe in the thought of Matryosha killing herself, even though it seems that it was at the back of his mind "all the time"? (172) Why, instead of trying to stop her, does he alternate between wanting to note everything carefully and losing himself in the contemplation of the tiny red spider? (171–173)

10. Does Stavrogin deliberately bring about Matryosha's suicide to keep his crime a secret?

Suggested textual analysis
Pages 171–173: beginning, "I had lunch in a pub," and ending, "but not so dark as to prevent me at last from seeing what I wanted. . . ."

Why does Stavrogin's dream about the painting of Acis and Galatea cause him to experience a change of heart and feel remorse for his ill treatment of Matryosha?

1. Why does Stavrogin buy a photograph of a girl who looks like Matryosha, but then leave it untouched and ultimately forget it? Why, before the dream, is Stavrogin able to make the "whole pile" of his memories obediently disappear whenever he wants? (176)

2. Why does Stavrogin make a special trip to the Dresden gallery to see the painting of Acis and Galatea? Why doesn't he connect the painting with Matryosha until it reappears to him in a dream? (177–178)

3. Why does Stavrogin have his dream after he has absent-mindedly gone to the wrong town? Why does the painting appear to him in the dream "not as a painting, but as a fact"? (176–177)

4. Why does Stavrogin think of the painting of the lovers as "The Golden Age"? Why does he associate "the cradle of European civilization" and "man's paradise on earth" with a peasant girl he has mistreated? (177)

5. Why does Stavrogin think of the dream as a "sublime illusion," but one for which mankind has "sacrificed everything" and "without which nations will not live and cannot even die"? Why does the dream make him shed tears for the first time in his life and have a sensation of happiness that he has never experienced before? (177–178)

6. Why, when Stavrogin tries to bring back the vanished dream, does he see in the center of the light the image of the tiny red spider that he had watched while Matryosha was hanging herself? (178)

7. Why does Stavrogin wish that the image of Matryosha called up by the dream could be "a real phantom"? Why does he wish that he could see "her real self, even if it were a hallucination"? (178)

8. Why is it the image of "a helpless creature with an unformed mind" threatening him that Stavrogin finds particularly distressing? (178)

9. Why does Stavrogin say he does not know and cannot tell to this day "whether this is what is called remorse or repentance"? (178)

10. Why is it that Stavrogin cannot help summoning up Matryosha's image, even though he cannot live with it and has the power to dismiss it? Why does he insist that he will continue to do so until he lapses into madness? (178–179)

Suggested textual analysis
Pages 177–178: beginning, "I had quite an extraordinary dream," and ending, "even if it were a hallucination!"

Why does Stavrogin bring his confession to Tikhon instead of publishing it as he had originally planned?

1. Why does Stavrogin resolve to confess on a grand scale by publishing three hundred copies of his confession? (179)

2. Why does Stavrogin tell Tikhon that if one man reads his confession he will not conceal it any longer and it will be read by everyone? (162)

3. Why does Stavrogin want to hear the passage from Revelation that begins, "And unto the angel of the church of the Laodicean write"? Why, after Tikhon's recitation, does Stavrogin tell him that he loves him very much? (160–161)

4. Why does Stavrogin insist that he was in control of himself and fully responsible for his actions when he committed his crime? Why does he say that he is making his statement in order to prove that he is in full possession of his mental faculties and realizes his position? (165, 173, 179)

5. Why does Stavrogin want everyone to look at him? Why does he say that he is falling back on this as his "last resource"? (179–180)

6. Are we meant to agree with Tikhon's suggestion that Stavrogin deliberately portrays himself as worse than he is? Why does Tikhon say that the confession is "a proud challenge by an accused to the judge"? (181)

7. Why does Stavrogin suggest to Tikhon that he may have lied in his confession? (182–183)

8. Why does Stavrogin admit that he would feel better if a complete stranger, rather than someone he respects or fears, forgave him inwardly? Why does he say that he would also feel much better if Tikhon forgave him? (183)

9. Why does Stavrogin insist that his chief and only purpose is to forgive himself? Why does he think "boundless suffering" will enable him to do this? (185)

Suggested textual analysis
Pages 158–162: beginning, "Do you believe in God?" and ending, "Tell me everything after you've read them."

Why does Tikhon think it would be a more suitable penance for Stavrogin to place himself under the guidance of an older and wiser monk than to make a public confession?

1. Why does Tikhon believe that, if Stavrogin follows his plan, it will be a "great sacrifice" that will enable Stavrogin to acquire everything he craves for and even what he does not expect? (186)

2. Why does Tikhon insist that the penance he has in mind is something quite different from the "real to goodness church penance" that Stavrogin scoffs at? (186)

3. Why does Tikhon say that "the absolute atheist stands on the last rung but one before most absolute faith (whether he steps higher or not), while an indifferent man has no faith at all"? (160)

4. Why does Tikhon say that Stavrogin's idea of publishing his confession is "a great idea" and "a Christian idea," but then suggest that it is not really repentance or Christian? (181)

5. Why does Tikhon think that Stavrogin is ashamed and afraid of repentance? (181)

6. Why is Tikhon less horrified by Stavrogin's crime itself than by "the vast unused energy that was deliberately spent on some abomination"? Why does he say that crimes such as Stavrogin's are common, but that it is extremely rare for someone to feel the whole depth of his degradation as Stavrogin does? (182)

7. Why does Tikhon think that Stavrogin would not be able to bear the universal laughter his confession would provoke—that the laughter would be "almost an impassable abyss"? (183–184)

8. Why does Tikhon say that if Stavrogin believes he can forgive himself and obtain that forgiveness for himself in this world through suffering, then he believes in everything already? (185–186) Why does Tikhon say, "God will forgive you for your unbelief, for you respect the Holy Spirit without knowing Him"? (186)

9. Why does Tikhon foresee that Stavrogin will kill himself, and that he will do so solely in order to avoid the publication of his confession? (187)

10. Why does Stavrogin reject Tikhon's plan for his salvation? (187)

Suggested textual analysis
Pages 184–187: from "Why, even in the form of this great penance," to the end of the story.

FOR FURTHER REFLECTION

1. Does Tikhon have the right solution for Stavrogin?

2. Is Stavrogin's crime mitigated by his confession? Why is confession an important part of repentance?

3. Does art have the power to turn the human heart from evil?

4. Is it better to be cold than lukewarm, evil than indifferent?

5. Why do we sometimes derive pleasure from representing ourselves as worse than we really are? Why might someone revel in baseness?

POETRY

Samuel Taylor Coleridge

SAMUEL TAYLOR COLERIDGE (1772–1834)
was born in Devonshire and studied at
Cambridge. Coleridge met William Wordsworth
in 1795 and together they published *Lyrical
Ballads* (1798), generally considered to herald
the beginning of English literary Romanticism,
and in which "The Rime of the Ancient
Mariner" appears. Four years later, Coleridge
wrote "Dejection: An Ode," a farewell to
poetry. Opium addiction, a desperately unhappy
private life, and deteriorating health combined
to undermine his confidence and his capacity to
work effectively. Although Coleridge went on
to produce major work in literary criticism,
aesthetics, and philosophy, the great poetic gift
never returned. He was elected a fellow of the
Royal Society of Literature in 1824.

The Rime of the Ancient Mariner
In Seven Parts

Facile credo, plures esse Naturas invisibles quam visibiles in rerum universitate. Sed horum [*sic*] omnium familiam quis nobis enarrabit? et gradus et cognationes et discrimina et singulorum munera? Quid agunt? quae loca habitant? Harum rerum notitiam semper ambivit ingenium humanum, nunquam attigit. Juvat, interea, non diffiteor, quandoque in animo, in tabulâ, majoris et melioris mundi imaginem contemplari: ne mens assuefacta hodiernae vitae minutiis se contrahat nimis, et tota subsidat in pusillas cogitationes. Sed veritati interea invigilandum est, modusque servandus, ut certa ab incertis, diem a nocte, distinguamus.

—T. Burnet[1]

Part I

An ancient Mariner meeteth three Gallants bidden to a wedding feast, and detaineth one.

IT IS an ancient Mariner
And he stoppeth one of three.
—"By thy long gray beard and glittering eye,
Now wherefore stopp'st thou me?

The Bridegroom's doors are opened wide,
And I am next of kin;
The guests are met, the feast is set:
May'st hear the merry din."

---

1. [From *Archaeologiae Philosophiae*, 68. "I can easily believe that there are more invisible than visible beings in the universe. But of their families, degrees, connections, distinctions,

He holds him with his skinny hand,
"There was a ship," quoth he.
"Hold off! unhand me, graybeard loon!"
Eftsoons[2] his hand dropped he.

The Wedding Guest is
spellbound by the eye
of the old seafaring
man, and constrained
to hear his tale.

He holds him with his glittering eye—
The Wedding Guest stood still,
And listens like a three years' child:
The Mariner hath his will.

The Wedding Guest sat on a stone:
He cannot choose but hear;
And thus spake on that ancient man,
The bright-eyed Mariner.

"The ship was cheered, the harbor cleared,
Merrily did we drop
Below the kirk,[3] below the hill,
Below the lighthouse top.

The Mariner tells
how the ship sailed
southward with a
good wind and fair
weather, till it reached
the line.

The Sun came up upon the left,
Out of the sea came he!
And he shone bright, and on the right
Went down into the sea.

---

and functions, who shall tell us? How do they act? Where are they found? About such
matters the human mind has always circled without attaining knowledge. Yet I do not
doubt that sometimes it is well for the soul to contemplate as in a picture the image
of a larger and better world, lest the mind, habituated to the small concerns of daily life,
limit itself too much and sink entirely into trivial thinking. But meanwhile we must be on
watch for the truth, avoiding extremes, so that we may distinguish certain from uncertain,
day from night." Burnet was a seventeenth-century English theologian.]

2. [*eftsoons*: straightway.]

3. [*kirk*: church.]

Higher and higher every day,
Till over the mast at noon—"
The Wedding Guest here beat his breast,
For he heard the loud bassoon.

The Wedding Guest
heareth the bridal
music; but the
Mariner continueth
his tale.

The bride hath paced into the hall,
Red as a rose is she;
Nodding their heads before her goes
The merry minstrelsy.

The Wedding Guest he beat his breast,
Yet he cannot choose but hear;
And thus spake on that ancient man,
The bright-eyed Mariner.

The ship driven by a
storm toward the
South Pole.

"And now the STORM-BLAST came, and he
Was tyrannous and strong;
He struck with his o'ertaking wings,
And chased us south along.

With sloping masts and dipping prow,
As who pursued with yell and blow
Still treads the shadow of his foe,
And forward bends his head,
The ship drove fast, loud roared the blast,
And southward aye we fled.

And now there came both mist and snow,
And it grew wondrous cold:
And ice, mast-high, came floating by,
As green as emerald.

The land of ice,
and of fearful sounds
where no living thing
was to be seen.

And through the drifts the snowy clifts[4]
Did send a dismal sheen:
Nor shapes of men nor beasts we ken—
The ice was all between.

The ice was here, the ice was there,
The ice was all around:
It cracked and growled, and roared and howled,
Like noises in a swound![5]

Till a great sea bird,
called the Albatross,
came through the
snow-fog, and was
received with great
joy and hospitality.

At length did cross an Albatross,
Thorough the fog it came;
As if it had been a Christian soul,
We hailed it in God's name.

It ate the food it ne'er had eat,
And round and round it flew.
The ice did split with a thunder-fit;
The helmsman steered us through!

And lo! the Albatross
proveth a bird of
good omen, and
followeth the ship
as it returned
northward through
fog and floating ice.

And a good south wind sprung up behind;
The Albatross did follow,
And every day, for food or play,
Came to the mariners' hollo!

In mist or cloud, on mast or shroud,
It perched for vespers nine;
Whiles all the night, through fog-smoke white,
Glimmered the white Moon-shine."

The ancient Mariner
inhospitably killeth
the pious bird of
good omen.

"God save thee, ancient Mariner!
From the fiends, that plague thee thus!—
Why look'st thou so?"—With my crossbow
I shot the ALBATROSS.

---

4. [*clifts*: cliffs.]

5. [*swound*: swoon.]

Part II

The Sun now rose upon the right:
Out of the sea came he,
Still hid in mist, and on the left
Went down into the sea.

And the good south wind still blew behind,
But no sweet bird did follow,
Nor any day for food or play
Came to the mariners' hollo!

His shipmates cry out
against the ancient
Mariner, for killing
the bird of good luck.

And I had done a hellish thing,
And it would work 'em woe:
For all averred, I had killed the bird
That made the breeze to blow.
Ah wretch! said they, the bird to slay,
That made the breeze to blow!

But when the fog
cleared off, they
justify the same, and
thus make themselves
accomplices in the
crime.

Nor dim nor red, like God's own head,
The glorious Sun uprist:[6]
Then all averred, I had killed the bird
That brought the fog and mist.
'Twas right, said they, such birds to slay,
That bring the fog and mist.

The fair breeze
continues; the ship
enters the Pacific
Ocean, and sails
northward, even till it
reaches the Line.

The fair breeze blew, the white foam flew,
The furrow followed free;
We were the first that ever burst
Into that silent sea.

The ship hath been
suddenly becalmed.

Down dropped the breeze, the sails dropped down,
'Twas sad as sad could be;
And we did speak only to break
The silence of the sea!

---

6. [*uprist:* arose.]

All in a hot and copper sky,
The bloody Sun, at noon,
Right up above the mast did stand,
No bigger than the Moon.

Day after day, day after day,
We stuck, nor breath nor motion;
As idle as a painted ship
Upon a painted ocean.

*And the Albatross
begins to be avenged.*

Water, water, everywhere,
And all the boards did shrink;
Water, water, everywhere,
Nor any drop to drink.

The very deep did rot: O Christ!
That ever this should be!
Yea, slimy things did crawl with legs
Upon the slimy sea.

About, about, in reel and rout
The death-fires danced at night;
The water, like a witch's oils,
Burnt green, and blue and white.

*A Spirit had followed them;
one of the invisible inhabitants of this planet, neither
departed souls nor angels;
concerning whom the
learned Jew, Josephus, and
the Platonic Constant-
inopolitan, Michael Psellus,
may be consulted. They are
very numerous, and there
is no climate or element
without one or more.*

And some in dreams assuréd were
Of the Spirit that plagued us so;
Nine fathom deep he had followed us
From the land of mist and snow.

And every tongue, through utter drought,
Was withered at the root;
We could not speak, no more than if
We had been choked with soot.

The shipmates, in their sore distress, would fain throw the whole guilt on the ancient Mariner: in sign whereof they hang the dead sea bird round his neck.

Ah! well-a-day! what evil looks
Had I from old and young!
Instead of the cross, the Albatross
About my neck was hung.

Part III

There passed a weary time. Each throat
Was parched, and glazed each eye.
A weary time! a weary time!
How glazed each weary eye,
When looking westward, I beheld
A something in the sky.

The ancient Mariner beholdeth a sign in the element afar off.

At first it seemed a little speck,
And then it seemed a mist;
It moved and moved, and took at last
A certain shape, I wist.[7]

A speck, a mist, a shape, I wist!
And still it neared and neared:
As if it dodged a water sprite,
It plunged and tacked and veered.

At its nearer approach, it seemeth him to be a ship; and at a dear ransom he freeth his speech from the bonds of thirst.

With throats unslaked, with black lips baked,
We could nor laugh nor wail;
Through utter drought all dumb we stood!
I bit my arm, I sucked the blood,
And cried, A sail! a sail!

---

7. [*wist:* knew.]

With throats unslaked, with black lips baked,
Agape they heard me call:
A flash of joy;   Gramercy![8] they for joy did grin,
And all at once their breath drew in,
As they were drinking all.

And horror follows.
For can it be a ship   See! see! (I cried) she tacks no more!
that comes onward   Hither to work us weal;[9]
without wind or tide?   Without a breeze, without a tide,
She steadies with upright keel!

The western wave was all aflame.
The day was well nigh done!
Almost upon the western wave
Rested the broad bright Sun;
When that strange shape drove suddenly
Betwixt us and the Sun.

It seemeth him but the   And straight the Sun was flecked with bars,
skeleton of a ship.   (Heaven's Mother send us grace!)
As if through a dungeon grate he peered
With broad and burning face.

Alas! (thought I, and my heart beat loud)
And its ribs are   How fast she nears and nears!
seen as bars on   Are those *her* sails that glance in the Sun,
the face of the   Like restless gossameres?
setting Sun.

The Specter-   Are those *her* ribs through which the Sun
Woman and her   Did peer, as through a grate?
Deathmate, and   And is that Woman all her crew?
no other on board   Is that a DEATH? and are there two?
the skeleton ship.   Is DEATH that woman's mate?

---

8. [*gramercy:* thank heavens.]

9. [*weal:* benefit.]

Like vessel,
like crew!

Her lips were red, *her* looks were free,
Her locks were yellow as gold:
Her skin was as white as leprosy,
The Nightmare LIFE-IN-DEATH was she,
Who thicks man's blood with cold.

Death and Life-
in-Death have diced
for the ship's crew,
and she (the latter)
winneth the ancient
Mariner.

The naked hulk alongside came,
And the twain were casting dice;
"The game is done! I've won! I've won!"
Quoth she, and whistles thrice.

No twilight within
the courts of
the Sun.

The Sun's rim dips; the stars rush out:
At one stride comes the dark;
With far-heard whisper, o'er the sea,
Off shot the specter-bark.

At the rising of
the Moon,

We listened and looked sideways up!
Fear at my heart, as at a cup,
My lifeblood seemed to sip!
The stars were dim, and thick the night,
The steersman's face by his lamp gleamed white;
From the sails the dew did drip—
Till clomb above the eastern bar
The hornéd Moon, with one bright star
Within the nether tip.

One after another,

One after one, by the star-dogged Moon,
Too quick for groan or sigh,
Each turned his face with a ghastly pang,
And cursed me with his eye.

His shipmates drop
down dead.

Four times fifty living men,
(And I heard nor sigh nor groan)
With heavy thump, a lifeless lump,
They dropped down one by one.

But Life-in-Death
begins her work on
the ancient Mariner.

The souls did from their bodies fly—
They fled to bliss or woe!
And every soul, it passed me by,
Like the whizz of my crossbow!

Part IV

The Wedding Guest
feareth that a Spirit is
talking to him;

"I fear thee, ancient Mariner!
I fear thy skinny hand!
And thou art long, and lank, and brown,
As is the ribbed sea-sand.

I fear thee and thy glittering eye,
And thy skinny hand, so brown."—

But the ancient
Mariner assureth him
of his bodily life, and
proceedeth to relate
his horrible penance.

Fear not, fear not, thou Wedding Guest!
This body dropped not down.

Alone, alone, all, all alone,
Alone on a wide wide sea!
And never a saint took pity on
My soul in agony.

He despiseth the
creatures of the calm,

The many men, so beautiful!
And they all dead did lie:
And a thousand thousand slimy things
Lived on; and so did I.

And envieth that they
should live, and so
many lie dead.

I looked upon the rotting sea,
And drew my eyes away;
I looked upon the rotting deck,
And there the dead men lay.

I looked to heaven, and tried to pray;
But or ever a prayer had gushed,
A wicked whisper came, and made
My heart as dry as dust.

I closed my lids, and kept them close,
And the balls like pulses beat,
For the sky and the sea, and the sea and the sky
Lay like a load on my weary eye,
And the dead were at my feet.

But the curse liveth for him in the eye of the dead men.

The cold sweat melted from their limbs,
Nor rot nor reek did they:
The look with which they looked on me
Had never passed away.

An orphan's curse would drag to hell
A spirit from on high;
But oh! more horrible than that
Is the curse in a dead man's eye!
Seven days, seven nights, I saw that curse,
And yet I could not die.

The moving Moon went up the sky,
And nowhere did abide:
Softly she was going up,
And a star or two beside—

In his loneliness and fixedness he yearneth towards the journeying Moon, and the stars that still sojourn, yet still move onward; and everywhere the blue sky belongs to them, and is their appointed rest, and their native country and their own natural homes, which they enter unannounced, as lords that are certainly expected and yet there is a silent joy at their arrival.

Her beams bemocked the sultry main,
Like April hoar-frost spread;
But where the ship's huge shadow lay,
The charmèd water burnt alway
A still and awful red.

By the light of the Moon he
beholdeth God's creatures of
the great calm.

Beyond the shadow of the ship,
I watched the water snakes:
They moved in tracks of shining white,
And when they reared, the elfish light
Fell off in hoary flakes.

Within the shadow of the ship
I watched their rich attire:
Blue, glossy green, and velvet black,
They coiled and swam; and every track
Was a flash of golden fire.

Their beauty and
their happiness.

He blesseth them
in his heart.

O happy living things! no tongue
Their beauty might declare:
A spring of love gushed from my heart,
And I blessed them unaware:
Sure my kind saint took pity on me,
And I blessed them unaware.

The spell begins
to break.

The self-same moment I could pray;
And from my neck so free
The Albatross fell off, and sank
Like lead into the sea.

Part V

Oh sleep! it is a gentle thing,
Beloved from pole to pole!
To Mary Queen the praise be given!
She sent the gentle sleep from Heaven,
That slid into my soul.

By grace of the holy Mother, the ancient Mariner is refreshed with rain.

The silly[10] buckets on the deck,
That had so long remained,
I dreamt that they were filled with dew;
And when I awoke, it rained.

My lips were wet, my throat was cold,
My garments all were dank;
Sure I had drunken in my dreams,
And still my body drank.

I moved, and could not feel my limbs:
I was so light—almost
I thought that I had died in sleep,
And was a blesséd ghost.

He heareth sounds and seeth strange sights and commotions in the sky and the element.

And soon I heard a roaring wind:
It did not come anear;
But with its sound it shook the sails,
That were so thin and sere.

The upper air burst into life!
And a hundred fire-flags sheen,[11]
To and fro they were hurried about!
And to and fro, and in and out,
The wan stars danced between.

And the coming wind did roar more loud,
And the sails did sigh like sedge;[12]
And the rain poured down from one black cloud;
The Moon was at its edge.

---

10. [*silly*: lowly, harmless.]

11. [*sheen*: shone.]

12. [*sedge*: rushlike plants bordering streams and lakes.]

The thick black cloud was cleft, and still
The Moon was at its side:
Like waters shot from some high crag,
The lightning fell with never a jag,
A river steep and wide.

*The bodies of the
ship's crew are
inspirited, and the
ship moves on;*

The loud wind never reached the ship,
Yet now the ship moved on!
Beneath the lightning and the Moon
The dead men gave a groan.

They groaned, they stirred, they all uprose,
Nor spake, nor moved their eyes;
It had been strange, even in a dream,
To have seen those dead men rise.

The helmsman steered, the ship moved on;
Yet never a breeze up-blew;
The mariners all 'gan work the ropes,
Where they were wont to do;
They raised their limbs like lifeless tools—
We were a ghastly crew.

The body of my brother's son
Stood by me, knee to knee:
The body and I pulled at one rope,
But he said nought to me.

*But not by the souls
of the men, nor by
demons of earth
or middle air, but by
a blessèd troop of
angelic spirits,
sent down by the
invocation of the
guardian saint.*

"I fear thee, ancient Mariner!"
Be calm, thou Wedding Guest!
'Twas not those souls that fled in pain,
Which to their corses[13] came again,
But a troop of spirits blest:

---

13. [*corses:* corpses.]

For when it dawned—they dropped their arms,
And clustered round the mast;
Sweet sounds rose slowly through their mouths,
And from their bodies passed.

Around, around, flew each sweet sound,
Then darted to the Sun;
Slowly the sounds came back again,
Now mixed, now one by one.

Sometimes a-dropping from the sky
I heard the sky-lark sing;
Sometimes all little birds that are,
How they seemed to fill the sea and air
With their sweet jargoning![14]

And now 'twas like all instruments,
Now like a lonely flute;
And now it is an angel's song,
That makes the heavens be mute.

It ceased; yet still the sails made on
A pleasant noise till noon,
A noise like of a hidden brook
In the leafy month of June,
That to the sleeping woods all night
Singeth a quiet tune.

Till noon we quietly sailed on,
Yet never a breeze did breathe:
Slowly and smoothly went the ship,
Moved onward from beneath.

---

14. [*jargoning:* warbling.]

The lonesome Spirit
from the South Pole
carries on the ship as
far as the Line, in
obedience to the
angelic troop, but still
requireth vengeance.

Under the keel nine fathom deep,
From the land of mist and snow,
The spirit slid: and it was he
That made the ship to go.
The sails at noon left off their tune,
And the ship stood still also.

The Sun, right up above the mast,
Had fixed her to the ocean:
But in a minute she 'gan stir,
With a short uneasy motion—
Backwards and forwards half her length
With a short uneasy motion.

Then like a pawing horse let go,
She made a sudden bound:
It flung the blood into my head,
And I fell down in a swound.

The Polar Spirit's
fellow demons, the
invisible inhabitants
of the element, take
part in his wrong;
and two of them relate,
one to the other, that
penance long and
heavy for the ancient
Mariner hath been
accorded to the Polar
Spirit, who returneth
southward.

How long in that same fit I lay,
I have not[15] to declare;
But ere my living life returned,
I heard and in my soul discerned
Two voices in the air.

"Is it he?" quoth one, "Is this the man?
By him who died on cross,
With his cruel bow he laid full low
The harmless Albatross.

The spirit who bideth by himself
In the land of mist and snow,
He loved the bird that loved the man
Who shot him with his bow."

---

15. [*have not:* cannot.]

The other was a softer voice,
As soft as honey-dew:
Quoth he, "The man hath penance done,
And penance more will do."

Part VI

FIRST VOICE

"But tell me, tell me! speak again,
Thy soft response renewing—
What makes that ship drive on so fast?
What is the ocean doing?"

SECOND VOICE

"Still as a slave before his lord,
The ocean hath no blast;
His great bright eye most silently
Up to the Moon is cast—

If he may know which way to go;
For she guides him smooth or grim.
See, brother, see! how graciously
She looketh down on him."

FIRST VOICE

The Mariner hath been cast into a trance; for the angelic power causeth the vessel to drive northward faster than human life could endure.

"But why drives on that ship so fast,
Without or wave or wind?"

SECOND VOICE

"The air is cut away before,
And closes from behind.

Fly, brother, fly! more high, more high!
Or we shall be belated:
For slow and slow that ship will go,
When the Mariner's trance is abated."

The supernatural motion is retarded; the Mariner awakes, and his penance begins anew.

I woke, and we were sailing on
As in a gentle weather:
'Twas night, calm night, the moon was high;
The dead men stood together.

All stood together on the deck,
For a charnel-dungeon fitter:
All fixed on me their stony eyes,
That in the Moon did glitter.

The pang, the curse, with which they died,
Had never passed away:
I could not draw my eyes from theirs,
Nor turn them up to pray.

The curse is finally expiated.

And now this spell was snapped: once more
I viewed the ocean green,
And looked far forth, yet little saw
Of what had else been seen—

Like one, that on a lonesome road
Doth walk in fear and dread,
And having once turned round walks on,
And turns no more his head;
Because he knows, a frightful fiend
Doth close behind him tread.

But soon there breathed a wind on me,
Nor sound nor motion made:
Its path was not upon the sea,
In ripple or in shade.

It raised my hair, it fanned my cheek
Like a meadow-gale of spring—
It mingled strangely with my fears,
Yet it felt like a welcoming.

Swiftly, swiftly flew the ship,
Yet she sailed softly too:
Sweetly, sweetly blew the breeze—
On me alone it blew.

And the ancient Mariner beholdeth his native country.

Oh! dream of joy! is this indeed
The lighthouse top I see?
Is this the hill? is this the kirk?
Is this mine own countree?

We drifted o'er the harbor-bar,
And I with sobs did pray—
O let me be awake, my God!
Or let me sleep alway.

The harbor-bay was clear as glass,
So smoothly it was strewn!
And on the bay the moonlight lay,
And the shadow of the Moon.

The rock shone bright, the kirk no less,
That stands above the rock:
The moonlight steeped in silentness
The steady weathercock.

The angelic spirits leave the dead bodies,

And the bay was white with silent light,
Till rising from the same,
Full many shapes, that shadows were,
In crimson colors came.

A little distance from the prow
Those crimson shadows were:

*And appear in their
own forms of light.*

I turned my eyes upon the deck—
Oh, Christ! what saw I there!

Each corse lay flat, lifeless and flat,
And, by the holy rood![16]
A man all light, a seraph[17]-man,
On every corse there stood.

This seraph-band, each waved his hand:
It was a heavenly sight!
They stood as signals to the land,
Each one a lovely light;

This seraph-band, each waved his hand,
No voice did they impart—
No voice; but oh! the silence sank
Like music on my heart.

But soon I heard the dash of oars,
I heard the Pilot's cheer;
My head was turned perforce away
And I saw a boat appear.

The Pilot and the Pilot's boy,
I heard them coming fast:
Dear Lord in Heaven! it was a joy
The dead men could not blast.

---

16. [*rood*: cross of Christ.]

17. [*seraph*: angel-like.]

I saw a third—I heard his voice:
It is the Hermit good!
He singeth loud his godly hymns
That he makes in the wood.
He'll shrieve[18] my soul, he'll wash away
The Albatross's blood.

Part VII

*The Hermit of
the Wood*

This Hermit good lives in that wood
Which slopes down to the sea.
How loudly his sweet voice he rears!
He loves to talk with marineres
That come from a far countree.

He kneels at morn, and noon, and eve—
He hath a cushion plump:
It is the moss that wholly hides
The rotted old oak stump.

The skiff-boat neared: I heard them talk,
"Why, this is strange, I trow!
Where are those lights so many and fair,
That signal made but now?"

*Approacheth the ship
with wonder.*

"Strange, by my faith!" the Hermit said—
"And they answered not our cheer!
The planks looked warped! and see those sails,
How thin they are and sere!
I never saw aught like to them,
Unless perchance it were

---

18. [*shrieve*: shrive; set free from sin.]

Brown skeletons of leaves that lag
My forest-brook along;
When the ivy tod[19] is heavy with snow,
And the owlet whoops to the wolf below,
That eats the she-wolf's young."

"Dear Lord! it hath a fiendish look,"
The Pilot made reply,
"I am a-feared"—"Push on, push on!"
Said the Hermit cheerily.

The boat came closer to the ship,
But I nor spake nor stirred;
The boat came close beneath the ship,
And straight a sound was heard.

The ship suddenly sinketh.

Under the water it rumbled on,
Still louder and more dread:
It reached the ship, it split the bay;
The ship went down like lead.

The ancient Mariner is saved in the Pilot's boat.

Stunned by that loud and dreadful sound,
Which sky and ocean smote,
Like one that hath been seven days drowned
My body lay afloat;
But swift as dreams, myself I found
Within the Pilot's boat.

Upon the whirl, where sank the ship,
The boat spun round and round;
And all was still, save that the hill
Was telling of the sound.

---

19. [*tod*: bushy clump.]

I moved my lips—the Pilot shrieked
And fell down in a fit;
The holy Hermit raised his eyes,
And prayed where he did sit.

I took the oars: the Pilot's boy,
Who now doth crazy go,
Laughed loud and long, and all the while
His eyes went to and fro.
"Ha! ha!" quoth he, "full plain I see,
The Devil knows how to row."

And now, all in my own countree,
I stood on the firm land!
The Hermit stepped forth from the boat,
And scarcely he could stand.

The ancient Mariner earnestly entreateth the Hermit to shrieve him; and the penance of life falls on him.

"O shrieve me, shrieve me, holy man!"
The Hermit crossed[20] his brow.
"Say quick," quoth he, "I bid thee say—
What manner of man art thou?"

Forthwith this frame of mine was wrenched
With a woeful agony,
Which forced me to begin my tale;
And then it left me free.

And ever and anon throughout his future life an agony constraineth him to travel from land to land;

Since then, at an uncertain hour,
That agony returns:
And till my ghastly tale is told,
This heart within me burns.

---

20. [*crossed*: made the sign of the cross upon.]

I pass, like night, from land to land;
I have strange power of speech;
That moment that his face I see,
I know the man that must hear me:
To him my tale I teach.

What loud uproar bursts from that door!
The wedding guests are there:
But in the garden-bower the bride
And bridemaids singing are:
And hark the little vesper bell,
Which biddeth me to prayer!

O Wedding Guest! this soul hath been
Alone on a wide wide sea:
So lonely 'twas, that God himself
Scarce seeméd there to be.

O sweeter than the marriage feast,
'Tis sweeter far to me,
To walk together to the kirk
With a goodly company!

To walk together to the kirk,
And all together pray,
While each to his great Father bends,
Old men, and babes, and loving friends
And youths and maidens gay!

And to teach, by his own example, love and reverence to all things that God made and loveth.

Farewell, farewell! but this I tell
To thee, thou Wedding Guest!
He prayeth well, who loveth well
Both man and bird and beast.

He prayeth best, who loveth best
All things both great and small;
For the dear God who loveth us,
He made and loveth all.

The Mariner, whose eye is bright,
Whose beard with age is hoar,
Is gone: and now the Wedding Guest
Turned from the bridegroom's door.

He went like one that hath been stunned,
And is of sense forlorn:[21]
A sadder and a wiser man,
He rose the morrow morn.

Samuel Taylor Coleridge

---

21. [*forlorn:* deprived.]

INTERPRETIVE QUESTIONS
FOR DISCUSSION

Why does blessing the water snakes free the Mariner from the curse imposed on him for killing the Albatross?

1. Why does the Mariner shoot the Albatross? (200)

2. Why does killing the Albatross bring down a curse on the Mariner and his shipmates? Why does the Spirit from the South Pole want to avenge the bird's death? (202)

3. Are the Mariner's shipmates punished for his sin or for their own fickleness toward the Albatross? (201)

4. Why does the author have Life-in-Death win over Death in the dice game for possession of the ancient Mariner? Why is the Mariner the only person on the ship whose life is spared? (205)

5. Why does a "wicked whisper" prevent the Mariner from praying? (207)

6. Why do the Mariner's comrades curse him in death as well as in life? (207)

7. Why does the Mariner think the water snakes are beautiful and bless them? Why does he do so "unaware"? (208)

8. After blessing the water snakes, why does the Mariner regain the ability to pray? Why does the Albatross fall from around his neck? (208)

Suggested textual analysis
Page 208: beginning, "Beyond the shadow of the ship," and ending, "Like lead into the sea."

Why is it a part of the ancient Mariner's penance that he must tell his story to strangers?

1. Why isn't the suffering that the Mariner endures before blessing the water snakes enough of a penance for his sin? (213)

2. Why, when they come to the Mariner's aid, do the angelic spirits inhabit the bodies of his dead comrades? (210)

3. Why does the Mariner have to endure the curse of his dead comrades one last time? (214)

4. Why does the ancient Mariner need the Hermit—an ordinary mortal—to complete the penance begun by the spirits? (217)

5. Why are we told that the Pilot and the Pilot's boy are driven mad by the sight of the Mariner coming to and taking the oars? Why is the Hermit not driven mad? (218–219)

6. Why does "the penance of life" fall on the Mariner at the moment he asks the Hermit to shrive him? Why, when asked to shrive the Mariner, does the Hermit ask him "what manner of man" he is? (219)

7. Why must the Mariner confess his tale not once, but over and over? Why must he experience agony until he has done so? (219)

Suggested textual analysis
Pages 217–220: beginning, "This Hermit good lives in that wood," and ending, "To him my tale I teach."

After hearing the Mariner's tale, why is the Wedding Guest both "a sadder and a wiser man"?

1. Why does the ancient Mariner choose someone on his way to a wedding feast to hear his tale? How does the Mariner know to whom he must tell his tale? (220)

2. Why is the ancient Mariner able to hold the Wedding Guest with his eye, though not with his hand? Why is it that the Wedding Guest "cannot choose but hear"? (198)

3. Why does the author have the Wedding Guest need to be reminded that he doesn't have to fear the ancient Mariner? (206, 210)

4. Why does the Mariner tell the Wedding Guest that he now finds the marriage feast less sweet than praying in church? (220)

5. What does the Mariner mean when he tells the Wedding Guest, "He prayeth best, who loveth best / All things both great and small"? (221)

6. Why does the author have the Wedding Guest turn from the bridegroom's door as a result of listening to the Mariner's tale? (221)

7. Why is the Wedding Guest "stunned" by the tale, even though the Mariner is the one who experienced its horror? Are we meant to think that the lesson learned by the Wedding Guest is the same as that learned by the Mariner? (221)

8. If the message of the Mariner's tale is one of love and forgiveness, why does it leave the Wedding Guest feeling sad?

Suggested textual analysis
Pages 220–221: from "I pass, like night, from land to land;" to the end of the poem.

FOR FURTHER REFLECTION

1. Do we need to do penance to free ourselves from guilt?

2. Is love for all creatures necessary to our spiritual well-being?

3. Why do people sometimes commit acts of violence or cruelty for no reason? Is a gratuitous crime worse than a calculated one?

4. Is the Mariner's punishment out of proportion to his crime?

5. Does becoming wiser make us sadder?

Questions for

COUP DE GRÂCE

Marguerite Yourcenar

MARGUERITE YOURCENAR (1903–1987)
was born Marguerite de Crayencour in
Brussels, of wealthy and cultured
Franco-Belgian parents. A novelist, poet,
playwright, and essayist, Yourcenar wrote
only in French but lived many years in the
United States, becoming a U.S. citizen in
1947. Educated entirely at home, Yourcenar
drew on her vast erudition to compose
wide-ranging essays and historical novels.
She is particularly known for her novel
Memoirs of Hadrian (1954), a fictional
autobiography of the second-century
Roman emperor. Yourcenar's extensive
body of work also includes French
translations of Greek poetry, black
spirituals, and the novels of Virginia Woolf
and Henry James. In 1980, Yourcenar
became the first woman to be elected to
the Académie Française.

NOTE: All page references are from The Noonday
Press edition of *Coup de Grâce* (first printing 1981).

INTERPRETIVE QUESTIONS
FOR DISCUSSION

Why is Erick unable to overcome his dislike of women and return Sophie's love?

1. Why is Erick convinced that friendship alone affords certitude? Why does he suggest that friendship is distinguished from love by "respect" and "total acceptance of another being"? (19)

2. Why does the relatively sophisticated and mature Erick lack the courage to talk to Sophie about her rape by the Lithuanian sergeant? Why does Erick's sense of Sophie as sexually "sullied" bring her closer to him? (28)

3. Why does Erick feel bound by a pact to Conrad? Why does this pact, and the fact that Sophie is Conrad's sister, prevent Erick from succumbing to Sophie's seduction? (59)

4. Why is Erick less uneasy than usual in Sophie's presence when she lies drunk on her bed, reminding him of "comrades attended in the same sorry state, and of Conrad himself"? (67)

5. Why does Erick feel, after standing on the lit balcony with Sophie when a bomb falls nearby, that these moments were like a solemn "exchange of vows" between them? (75)

6. Why is Sophie finally able to bring herself to embrace Erick? Why does Erick say that she fell on his breast "as if she were reeling from a wound"? (76)

7. Why is Erick able to accept Sophie's embrace and to kiss her mouth and hair? Why does he say that they were both "innocent as beings just resurrected"? (76)

8. Why does the ecstasy of embracing Sophie turn to horror for Erick, releasing in him the childhood memory of a starfish that his mother had forced into his hand on the beach? (76–77)

9. Why, after Erick and Sophie's embrace, is it as if one of them is already dead—Erick in what concerned Sophie, and Sophie "in that part of herself which had ventured to hope" because she loved Erick? (77)

10. Why does Erick feel "impelled" to ask himself whether he loved Sophie? Why does he imagine how "it would have been good to begin all over again somewhere with her alone, like two sole survivors of a shipwreck"? (88–89)

11. Why does Erick view his need for solitude, rather than a "love for boys," as the source of his homosexual attachments? (92)

12. Why is Erick prepared to pledge himself to Sophie, despite his belief that women play havoc with the solitude he must have? (92–93)

Suggested textual analyses
Pages 73–77: beginning, " 'Often,' she said, coming closer to me," and ending, "that part of herself which had ventured to hope because she loved me."

Pages 88–93: beginning, "That night my pacing from window to wardrobe," and ending, "an interval which could prove to be that of death itself."

Why do Sophie and Erick play out the roles of victim and executioner?

1. Why does Erick characterize Sophie's pursuit of him as a "game" in which one of them is the leader? (31) Why are we told that Erick thinks of Sophie as a vast country that he "subdued"? (76)

2. Why is Erick drawn to Sophie's courage and incorruptibility, qualities that he views as dangerous in the same way that fire, whose law is "to burn, or to die," is dangerous? (38)

3. Why does Sophie's "uprightness"—her integrity—take the form of self-hate when Erick rejects her love? Why does she conclude that she is "beneath contempt" in offering herself to Erick? (44)

4. Why does Sophie persist in loving the cold, unresponsive Erick? Why are we told that she touched Erick with "slight, discouraged gestures which were less a caress than the motion of someone blind"? (62; cf. 44)

5. Why does Erick humiliate himself by knocking on Sophie's door when he knows she is inside with his rival, Volkmar, and later slap her when he sees her defiantly kiss Volkmar at the Christmas party? (82, 86) Why does Sophie call Erick her "only true friend" and beg his pardon for kissing Volkmar? (90)

6. Why does Erick doubt that he would have done anything to prevent Sophie's departure from Kratovitsy even if he had known the circumstances of their final meeting? (108)

7. Why does Erick maintain that he had only "a secondary part" in Sophie's execution, that "after a certain moment it was Sophie who took over the command of her own destiny . . . the initiative for her death"? (135)

8. Seeing Sophie "clothed" for him "with the twofold prestige of a soldier and of a woman about to die," why does Erick feel inclined to stammer "some incoherent words of affection"? Why is Erick convinced that Sophie would have rejected with scorn any words of affection from him? (145)

9. Why does Sophie tell Erick, when he repeats that he will do his "best," "Don't try any more. . . . It doesn't suit you"? (145–146)

10. Why does Sophie insist that Erick be her executioner? Why does Erick end up placing his honor above his wish to spare Sophie's life? (146–147)

11. Why does Sophie unbutton the upper half of her jacket at her execution, as if Erick were going to press his revolver against her heart? (150)

12. Why does Erick conclude that it was revenge, not love, that motivated Sophie's request that he be the one to shoot her? (151) Are we meant to think that he is right?

Suggested textual analyses

Pages 33–42: beginning, "How could one not play, holding all the cards?" and ending, "since we agreed in treating Conrad like a child."

Pages 140–151: from "Sophie came next, ushered in by two soldiers," to the end of the novel.

After losing Sophie and Conrad, why does Erick choose the solitary life of a mercenary?

1. Why is Erick compelled to tell his story, the "interminable confession" that, in reality, he is making to "no one but himself"? (5)

2. Why are we told that Erick became a soldier of fortune who took part in the "various movements in Central Europe which culminated in the rise of Hitler"? (4) Why does it turn out that Conrad and Sophie die for their diametrically opposed political views while Erick survives to fight for causes in which he does not believe?

3. Why is Erick willing to risk his life only for causes he does not believe in? Why does Erick view himself as morally impotent? (9)

4. Why does Erick, who lacks all interest in political causes, believe that if he hadn't reported for military duty during World War I he would have "failed to live up to what was . . . most decent" in him? (15)

5. Why does Conrad represent for Erick "a fixed point, a center, a heart"? (10) Why does Erick think of Conrad as an "exquisite soul"? (34)

6. Why does Erick believe that the happiness he knew at Kratovitsy with Conrad during World War I was "the real thing, the inalterable gold piece"? Why does Erick say that "to have once possessed such happiness leaves one proof against vague philosophizing; it helps to simplify life"? (14)

7. When Erick identifies Kratovitsy with a "certain ideal of happiness," why does he also think of the period after Sophie's disappearance, when Kratovitsy was once again like "an outpost of the Teutonic Order, a frontier fortress of the Livonian Brothers of the Sword"? (124)

8. In watching Conrad die, why does Erick fear most that Conrad's courage might suddenly fail him? (128–129) Why does Erick emphasize that it was Conrad "who made unforgettable that mixture of destitution and grandeur" in their retreat from Kratovitsy? (127)

9. Why is the handful of men that Erick led in retreat the only group to whom he "ever felt bound by strong human ties"? (128)

10. What are we meant to think of Erick's view that Conrad's death in battle was a "happy chance," sparing him what the future would bring? (131)

11. Why are we told that, before shooting Sophie, Erick momentarily feels regret for her unborn children, "who would have inherited her courage and her eyes"? (150)

12. Why does the author have Erick end his story with the misogynistic assertion that "one is always trapped, somehow, in dealings with women"? (151)

Suggested textual analyses

Pages 9–16: beginning, "Furthermore, whatever the dangers an adventurer chooses to face," and ending, "to a totally empty future."

Pages 123–131: beginning, "From that time on, Sophie was as dead and buried," and ending, "such a death was a happy chance."

FOR FURTHER REFLECTION

1. Do you think Yourcenar is being entirely candid—with herself or with her readers—when she insists in the last sentence of her preface to *Coup de Grâce* that the novel must be read as a human, and not a political, document?

2. Do you agree with Yourcenar's defense of Erick's character in her preface to *Coup de Grâce*—that is, that he has an "intrinsic nobility"? Is the author's dismissal of Erick's anti-Semitism— as simply the "habitual irony" of an aristocrat toward Jews— legitimate?

3. Are we better or worse off for having lost the chivalric code of conduct that died with the caste and world of Erick von Lhomond and Conrad and Sophie de Reval?

4. If *Coup de Grâce* is a tragedy as the author says, what is Erick's tragic flaw?

5. Is Erick's particular brand of glorification of war and death still with us in our post-Hiroshima world? Do the "chivalric dreams of comradeship" that Erick exalts still have the power to pull young people into war, or have we outgrown this ideal?

Questions for

PHILADELPHIA FIRE

John Edgar Wideman

JOHN EDGAR WIDEMAN (1941–   )
is perhaps best known for his memoir,
Brothers and Keepers, and for his novels and
short stories set in Homewood, the black
neighborhood in Pittsburgh where he spent
the first ten years of his life. In 1963, he
became only the second African American
to win a Rhodes scholarship. After studying
literature at Oxford University, he returned to
the United States to teach and write. In 1968,
at the request of two students, he taught a
course on African American literature, which
led him to new directions in his writing.
Moving away from a primarily white literary
tradition to embrace multiple traditions—
"European and Afro-American, the Academy
and the Street"—he forged his own language
for describing the violent experiences and
inner lives of his characters, which include
members of his own family. (Wideman's
brother and son have both been sentenced to
life in prison for murder.) Wideman received
the PEN/Faulkner Award twice, for *Sent for
You Yesterday* and *Philadelphia Fire.*

NOTE: All page references are from the First Vintage
Contemporaries edition (first printing 1991).

INTERPRETIVE QUESTIONS
FOR DISCUSSION

**Why does Cudjoe return from his exile in Mykonos to write the
story of the holocaust on Osage Avenue and of the lost boy, Simba?**

1. Why does Cudjoe believe that he must find Simba in order
   "to be whole again"? (8) Why does Cudjoe think of the boy
   who is the only survivor of the conflagration as "brother,
   son, a lost limb"? (7–8)

2. Why does Cudjoe say that in order to reach the boy, Simba,
   he must, "at the risk of turning to stone, look back at his own
   lost children"? (23)

3. When Caroline leaves him, why does Cudjoe remove himself
   absolutely from his sons' lives, telling himself it's "all or
   nothing"? (69)

4. Why were Cudjoe and Caroline never able to establish
   "dependable, easy, common ground"? Why was Cudjoe
   unfaithful to Caroline? (55)

5. Why does Cudjoe consider himself guilty of being a "half-black
   someone" for marrying a white woman and fathering half-white
   children? (9–10)

6. Why is Cudjoe angered by Caroline's habit of closing her robe or
   shutting her knees if she notices him peering between her naked
   legs? Why does he accuse her of hiding something from him?
   (56–58)

7. What does Cudjoe mean when he thinks to himself that he will tell Margaret Jones that "we're all in this together. . . . We are all trapped in the terrible jaws of something shaking the life out of us"? Why does he want to tell her that "he was lost but now he's found"? (22)

8. Why is Margaret Jones skeptical about the value of the book that Cudjoe wants to write about the fire? (19)

9. Is Margaret Jones speaking specifically to the black community when she accuses people of not caring about the destruction of the neighborhood and the murdered children of Osage Avenue? (19) Why does the author emphasize that it was the city's black administration who ordered that the bomb be dropped on 6221 Osage Avenue? (41–42, 81)

10. Why is hearing Simba's spirit voice tell how Simba and the other children must hide together "inside of night skin" the closest Cudjoe ever gets to the boy? (49–52)

11. Why does Cudjoe dream that he is on a basketball court where he is simultaneously rolling around on the ground with his legs chopped off at the knees, and floating upright, screaming and staring down at a boy lynched from the basketball rim? (93)

12. Why does Cudjoe refuse to invent in order to fill in the blank parts of his dream? What does he mean when he says that "the blanks are real," part of the dream? (94)

Suggested textual analyses
Pages 45–58: beginning, "Cudjoe decides he will think of himself," and ending, "He'd make her suffer for this."

Pages 91–94: beginning, "Timbo. Has anyone downtown," and ending, "Shit, man."

Why does the author say that Cudjoe's production of *The Tempest* is the central event of his narrative—sitting dead center, "the storm in the eye of the storm"?

1. What does the author mean when he says that Cudjoe's production of *The Tempest* "works like an engine, a heart in the story's chest . . . tying something to something else, that sign by which we know time's conspiring, expiring"? (133)

2. When we read about Cudjoe's rewritten version of *The Tempest*, are we meant to think of Sam on his island as a kind of Prospero, Cassandra as another Miranda, and the lusting Cudjoe as Caliban? (143–145)

3. Why does Cudjoe violate Sam's trust by secretly watching his daughter, Cassandra, shower in the moonlight? (65) Why does Cudjoe regard Sam as his twin? (64)

4. Why do we learn that Cudjoe voyeuristically watches the girl in Clark Park and his neighbor who walks around her apartment naked? (26, 54) Why does he prefer thinking of these women as having no name and no history—as "everywoman and no woman"? (54, 64)

5. Why does Cudjoe stage *The Tempest* so that both Miranda and Caliban are victims of that "lying ass wanna be patriarch Prospero" who, by identifying Caliban as beast, uses the paradigm of race to rationalize his colonization of Caliban's island? (140–142)

6. Is the author suggesting that race is at the root of Cudjoe's, as well as Caliban's, stunted ability to love?

7. Why does Timbo tell Cudjoe, "Everybody knows can't nobody free Caliban but his own damn self"? (145)

8. Why does Cudjoe, in reimagining *The Tempest,* identify the invasion of Caliban's island by Prospero with Caliban's dawning of consciousness—his discovery of loneliness, his newfound awareness of time and death? (146–148)

9. Why does Cudjoe run away from his feeling of responsibility for the children he taught? Why are we told that he always felt guilty about deserting them? (149–150)

10. Why does the author give "Kaliban's Kiddie Korps" as the alternate name for the Kids Krusade? (88) Are we meant to think that Cudjoe is partly responsible for the roving bands of kids and their brewing insurrection?

11. Why does the author say that this narrative is about "stopping time, catching time"? (133) Are we meant to be reminded of Cudjoe's penchant for stepping "out of time" by always writing about many places at once? (23)

12. Why does Cudjoe, who wants to run when the program for the dead of Osage Avenue is over, instead turn and face the mob he imagines is chasing him and "screaming for blood"? (198–199) Why does Cudjoe tell himself, *"Never again. Never again"?* (199)

Suggested textual analyses
Pages 130–145: beginning, "But be that as it may," and ending, "Everybody knows can't nobody free Caliban but his own damn self."

Pages 194–199: from "Cudjoe leans against the edge of a fountain," to the end of the novel.

Why does Wideman include autobiographical material about his own lost son in his novel about the Philadelphia fire and Cudjoe's search for Simba?

1. Why does the author, in telling us about "the nightmare of his son's pain," choose to identify his situation with that of Cudjoe and his son's situation with that of Simba? (111)

2. Why does the author think that, like Oedipus, he brought down calamity on himself? (104, 106)

3. Why does the author suggest that regaining his "narrative faculty" and completing his book about the fire might be contingent upon dealing with his son's "story"? (115)

4. Why does the author suggest a connection between his ill son and the ailing city by describing both as sinking into a profound, or terminal, "stupor"? (20, 116)

5. Why does the author juxtapose an account of the University's dismantling of its pragmatic Social Work program—its refusal to take responsibility for the "runaway chaos of an ailing urban landscape"—and his impassioned account of the state's refusal to accept responsibility for treatment of his son's mental illness? (111–116)

6. Why does the author think that he might be using his character Cudjoe to hide from himself? Why does he ask himself if Cudjoe is "mirror or black hole"? (122)

7. Why does the author suggest that Simba—the novel's fictional counterpart of his own lost son—joins the predatory gang of kids who call themselves Kaliban's Kiddie Korps? (50–52, 165–166) Why does Cudjoe dream that the children dress in white robes like Ku Klux Klanners? (52)

8. Why does the loss of a child alter for the author his sense of the "endless ebb, flow and possibility" of time? What does he mean when he says that "a child lost cancels the natural order, the circle is broken"? (119)

9. Why does the author, who feels that words between him and his son have become useless, stress his imprisoned son's need to "write a narrative of self"? (99, 110) Why does the author end Part Two of his novel with a plea to his son to live his life strongly by unfolding his days "one by one" and piecing together "a story that shapes" him? (150–151)

10. Are we meant to think that the author's declaration of profound and unalterable connection with his son is for him a new way of thinking about their relationship? (150)

Suggested textual analysis
Pages 108–120: "Arrived Maine Friday," and ending, "speaking to me a hundred times a day, every day."

Why does the author imagine that James Brown (or "King"), the dreadlocked leader who supposedly dies in the holocaust on Osage Avenue, is resurrected as a derelict only to be burned alive by children?

1. Why does J. B. prefer to be believed dead—to be "no one, no where"—rather than assist "survivors in the bar-b-qued city"? (184, 157) Why does he say that it's best to let the city, this "Black Camelot," burn? (159, 186)

2. Why are we told that as a student J. B. had loved an art history course, in which he could lie back, invisible in the darkened lecture hall, and practice "the art of letting the wide world pass him by"? (183)

3. Why does J. B. say that instead of running away from the "tragedy of a city burning," what is needed is "realism"— demographics, statistics, objectivity? (157)

4. What does J. B. mean when he tells himself, "In time a separation . . . between your own sorry self and the sorrows of the city could be effected"? (157)

5. Why are we told that the members of King's family become his "slaves," and that J. B. (the "King of Savers") fantasizes about women as sexual objects? (11, 178, 184–185)

6. Why does Richard Corey, a former member of King's family who betrayed King and his comrades to the police, decide to commit suicide? (174–175, 178–179) Why does Corey say that in squealing to the pigs he "betrayed our good mother Earth"? (167)

7. Why does the author stress the pleasure that bystanders take in witnessing Corey's suicide, and the confusion that they spread in "retailing the tale" of his death? (179, 180–181)

8. Why, in his final death hallucination, does J. B. think that it is "little white boys" who have drenched him with kerosene and set him on fire? (188)

9. Why are we told that the heat of the fire returns J. B. to his childhood, when sun was "hot as fire under the asphalt cooking his bare toes"? (189; c.f. 47)

10. Does the novel offer the hope that countless individuals like Cudjoe, by correct remembering and "seeing," can reshape the city's reality? (53–54, 199)

Suggested textual analyses

Pages 155–166: beginning, "The old town's dying behind J. B.'s back," and ending, "here to stay / here to stay."

Pages 179–189: beginning, "Because he skulked at the rear of the crowd," and ending, "you can always light a match."

FOR FURTHER REFLECTION

1. Is the violence that pervades American society rooted in race?

2. Does *Philadelphia Fire* suggest that personal responsibility and political responsibility are one and the same?

3. Do you agree with Timbo's view that young people in the sixties failed to effect lasting social change because they got bored with themselves and wanted to have a good time rather than shoulder the responsibilities of "grown-up business"?

4. What can we do to help inner-city youth survive in a world that is often alien, hostile, and chaotically violent? How can we help them to reimagine their lives—to construct "an identity, an ego, a life, an intimacy with who and what" they are?

5. How can Americans, both black and white, free themselves from what Wideman calls "the paradigm of race—a vision of humankind and society based on the premise that not all people are created equal and some are born with the right to exploit others"?

ACKNOWLEDGMENTS

All possible care has been taken to trace ownership and secure permission for each selection in this anthology. The Great Books Foundation wishes to thank the following authors, publishers, and representatives for permission to reprint copyrighted material.

After the Ball, by Leo Tolstoy, from THE PENGUIN BOOK OF RUSSIAN SHORT STORIES, edited by David Richards. Translated by Lesley Chamberlain. Copyright 1981 by Lesley Chamberlain. Reprinted by permission of Lesley Chamberlain.

On Evil, Guilt, and Power, from BEYOND GOOD AND EVIL, ON THE GENEALOGY OF MORALS, and THE WILL TO POWER, by Friedrich Nietzsche. BEYOND GOOD AND EVIL translated by Walter Kaufmann; copyright 1966 by Random House, Inc. ON THE GENEALOGY OF MORALS translated by Walter Kaufmann and R. J. Hollingdale; copyright 1967 by Random House, Inc. THE WILL TO POWER translated by Walter Kaufmann and R. J. Hollingdale; copyright 1967 by Walter Kaufmann. All reprinted by permission of Random House, Inc.

Moosbrugger, from THE MAN WITHOUT QUALITIES, by Robert Musil. Translated by Sophie Wilkins and Burton Pike. Copyright 1995 by Alfred A. Knopf, Inc. Reprinted by permission of Alfred A. Knopf, Inc.

The Sorcerer's Apprentice, from THE SORCERER'S APPRENTICE: TALES AND CONJURATIONS, by Charles Johnson. Copyright 1983 by Charles Johnson. Reprinted by permission of Scribner, a division of Simon & Schuster.